W9-CVW-895

Legal and Ethical Issues in Acquisitions

Forthcoming Topics in *The Acquisitions Librarian* series:

- Acquisitions Costs, Number 4, Jim Coffey, editor
- Evaluating Acquisitions and Collection Development, Number 5
- Acquisition Plans, Jobbers, Vendors, and Book Dealers, Number 6
- Acquisitions and Resource Sharing, Number 7
- Gifts and Exchanges, Number 8
- Serials Acquisitions, Number 9
- Acquisitions and Collection Development Policies, Number 10
- The Collections Manager, and Training of Acquisitions Librarians, Number 11
- Acquisitions of Popular Culture Materials, Number 12

Note: The order of the series is subject to change

Legal and Ethical Issues in Acquisitions

Katina Strauch
Bruce Strauch
Editors

The Haworth Press
New York • London

Legal and Ethical Issues in Acquisitions has also been published as *The Acquisitions Librarian*, Number 3, 1990.

The Haworth Press, Inc., 10 Alice Street, Binghamton, NY 13904-1580
EUROSPAN/Haworth, 3 Henrietta Street, London WC2E 8LU England

Library of Congress Cataloging-in-Publication Data

Legal and ethical issues in acquisitions / Katina Strauch, Bruce Strauch, guest editors.
    p.   cm.
"Has also been published as the Acquisitions librarian, volume 3, 1990" — Verso t.p.
Includes bibliographical references.
ISBN 1-56024-007-5 (acid free paper)
    1. Acquisitions (Libraries) — Moral and ethical aspects. 2. Library science — Moral and ethical aspects. 3. Library legislation — United States. 4. Librarians — Professional ethics. I. Strauch, Katina P., 1946 – . II. Strauch, Bruce.
Z689.L43   1990
025.2 – dc20
                                                  90-35841
                                                     CIP

Legal and Ethical Issues in Acquisitions

CONTENTS

ABOUT THE EDITORS

Katina Strauch, MLS, is Head, Collection Development at the College of Charleston Library. She has been an acquisitions/collection development librarian since 1979. Ms. Strauch received her Masters of Science in Library Science from the University of North Carolina at Chapel Hill.

Bruce Strauch, JD, MA, is professor of law and economics at the Citadel. He is also a practicing attorney. Dr. Strauch received his Masters in Economics from Oxford University, Oxford, England, and his Juris Doctor from the University of North Carolina at Chapel Hill.

Introduction

Katina Strauch
Bruce Strauch

Increasingly it is being recognized that acquisitions is a business. One of the largest budgets in the typical college or university is expended there in an ongoing process. Contracts are executed daily. Some are simple purchases; others are long-term agreements. Gifts are received and their value calculated for tax deductions. Trade customs, or the ordinary way of doing business, are evolving. The ethical element of trade customs is being fiercely debated, as both sides try to reach consensus on what is "fair."

What are some of the ramifications of the climate which practicing acquisitions librarians now find themselves in? What are some of the skills which will be required as the acquisitions librarian changes to meet the emerging demands?

This collection deals with some of the legal and ethical issues which we all face. The authors of many of the articles are not librarians, but lawyers, accountants and business men and women in the non-library environment.

As a lead off, William M. Hannay, a practicing lawyer, gives us an overview of some of the antitrust issues in publishing. The current trend of mergers and acquisitions in publishing is impacting our purchasing environment. What happens in the future in this area will be crucial to how we will do business in the future.

Suzanne Krebsbach, a law librarian, gives us a brief introduction to the Federal Trade Commission and its regulation of the publishing industry. As acquisitions librarians, we need to be aware of the controlling regulations and of the committees of our various professional associations which attempt to oversee relations between libraries and publishers.

A look at some more specific practices by publishers is the focus

1

of the next two papers. The first, by Margaret Axtmann, a law librarian, centers on the aspects of publisher advertising that are most useful to librarians and practices by publishers which make the acquisition of materials problematic. Marcie Kingsley and Philip Berwick, law librarians as well, center on billing practices by some publishers and the good and bad aspects of publisher invoicing. The useful, practical suggestions in both articles can be used as a guide by acquisitions librarians when communicating with publishers.

The next two articles deal with charitable contributions and the acquisitions librarians' role. The first article is by an acquisitions librarian who has a long history of dealing with charitable donations and the second article is by three tax accountants. In a meticulous and thoroughly researched article, Corrie Marsh tells us exactly what is necessary, especially if we are lucky enough to receive large non-cash charitable contributions. White, Morgan, and Gordon take a slightly different approach, centering on the possibilities of library fund-raising and the potential tax ramifications for donors. Perhaps as acquisitions librarians, we need to study these issues more closely as we move into an era when budgets are limited and prices are rising.

The purchase of new technologies, such as CD-ROM, is the focus of the next two papers, by Joyce Ogburn, an acquisitions librarian, and Meta Nissley, acquisitions and collection management librarian. Clearly the acquisition of this type of material is a growing activity for most libraries as users find them attractive since they allow end-user access. But, as both Ogborn and Nissley point out, we must be careful to recognize the issues involved in the acquisition of such materials and protect our libraries against practices by publishers that are not in our best interests.

Suzanne Freeman and Barbara Winters, collection management librarian and acquisitions librarian respectively, next discuss some ethical and fiscal problems associated with selecting and acquiring library materials in the current publishing climate. With the publication of materials increasing in both print and non-print, librarians must become more involved in the process of selection of the appropriate materials for their collections.

James Coffey, a Technical Services Librarian who has also worked as a vendor of library materials, gives us a view of the business relationship between libraries and booksellers. Stressing the necessity for librarians to become more cognizant of the way vendors operate is the focus of Coffey's article. Indeed, this fact is implied by the articles that precede and follow Coffey's.

Specific, nitty-gritty if you will, issues are the focus of the last four papers included in this issue. The first is by a lawyer, Bruce Strauch, who focuses on a problem in some academic libraries which may be near public or private high schools and which are regularly inundated with an influx of high school students, many of whom are juveniles. Just what are the legal ramifications of a library allowing access to materials which may be termed inappropriate for this age group?

In the next article, Barbara Carlson, a medical serials librarian, focuses on the claiming process for journals and some of the factors which make this a frustrating process and even pit publisher and librarian as adversaries. The impact of automation on this process is also explored.

N. Bernard "Buzzy" Basch and Judy McQueen have authored the third "nitty-gritty" article which is an enlightening discussion of subscription vendor service charges. Former president of a subscription agency, Basch is ably qualified to give us some "insider" information on how to get "the best deal" with regard to service charges.

The fourth and last article in this sequence is by Rosann Bazirjian, acquisitions/collection development librarian. This paper gives a philosophical base to a problem which many acquisitions librarians delay indefinitely, the weeding of books from the library's collections.

We have only begun to explore the many legal and ethical issues which impact on the acquisitions environment. But we believe we have made a good start!

Current Antitrust Issues in Publishing

William M. Hannay

SUMMARY. Mergers and pricing by publishers have had a significant place in the news over the past several years. This article discusses some of the antitrust laws and issues that have arisen and the role of competition in the application of antitrust laws.

MERGERS AND ACQUISITIONS

In a recent spy novel,[1] the entire plot revolves around sinister foreign interests acquiring control of a substantial share of the American broadcast and publishing media. A few years ago, the premise of such a plot would have been ludicrous, but no more. A number of financial commentators are predicting that five to eight giant corporations will dominate the world communications industry by the year 2000 or so.[2]

The trend is already unmistakable. In the last few years, Japan's Sony Corporation bought CBS Records; West Germany's Bertelsmann acquired RCA Records and the Doubleday and Bantam Books publishers, Robert Maxwell of Britain purchased the Macmillan publishing house, and Rupert Murdoch bought Triangle Publications and 20th Century Fox Film for his Australia-based News Corp. Most recently of all, Paramount Pictures and Warner Communications have fought over which one will merge with Time, Inc. to create the biggest media company in the world.[3]

This wave of "media globalization" raises serious questions about the political, social, and intellectual consequences of such consolidations.[4] For example, Ben Bagdikian, the former dean of

---

William M. Hannay is a partner in the Chicago-based law firm of Schiff, Hardin & Waite and an Adjunct Professor at IIT/Chicago-Kent College of Law in Chicago. He specializes in antitrust and trade regulation law.

the graduate school of journalism at the University of California at Berkeley, warns that the consequences are ultimately a threat to democracy. "We're not talking about the food industry or the soft-drink industry," he said. "There's something special about the media business. You're talking about the culture and political knowledge of the whole population. If we believe in the experience of our history, diversity is better than a monopoly of the few."[5]

For those concerned about fighting this trend towards concentration, the federal antitrust laws would be an important weapon to use. To date, however, they have not been so used. Why not? One critic of the merger and LBO craze blames it on the "Just Say Yes" antitrust policies of the 1980s. "Congress has not repealed the antitrust statutes," he notes. "However, for practical purposes the Reagan administration abrogated their effect by not enforcing them. As much as anything, this inaction created the climate for junk bonds, corporate raids, and the incessant trading, not of stocks, but of whole companies."[6]

The antitrust laws were written decades ago to control the exercise of private economic power by preventing monopoly, punishing cartels, and otherwise protecting competition.[7] The principal antitrust statute regulating mergers and acquisitions is Section 7 of the Clayton Act.[8] First enacted in 1914, this important statute was amended and expanded by the Celler-Kefauver Act in 1950. Section 7 provides that "No person engaged in commerce . . . shall acquire, directly or indirectly, . . . the stock or . . . assets of another person . . . , where in any line of commerce in any section of the country, the effect of such acquisition may be substantially to lessen competition, or to tend to create a monopoly."

While Congress used the word "may" to allow flexibility in applying this law, the statute explicitly focuses on the lessening of "competition." The key word in understanding the scope and purpose of the Clayton Act and the other antitrust laws is "competition." It is the protection of "competition" alone that motivates and limits the application of the antitrust laws. Other possible social goals such as preserving freedom of expression or encouraging creativity are simply not proper justifications for invoking the antitrust laws, however meritorious (or indeed vital) they may otherwise be.

Thus, if there is no probability that a merger will lessen *competition*, the transaction does not violate federal antitrust law.

The question then becomes what is meant by the term "competition" in Section 7. During the 1950s and 1960s, the courts gave a broad reading to the term based on the apparent purpose of the 1950 Congressional amendments to Section 7. In his classic treatise on antitrust law, Professor Lawrence Sullivan has described the purpose of those amendments, as follows:

> Congress was concerned in a very broad and general way about increases in business concentration. It was less a matter of having well formed theories about the changing structure of American industry than of a shared and general feeling of concern, even alarm, about the economic, social and political effects of the changes going on — if you will, about the processes of change themselves and about the reduction in local control of business as operating control of industry generally became more centered in the east. (L. Sullivan, *Antitrust* (1977) at 592)[9]

During the 1970s and 1980s, however, the federal enforcement agencies and some courts have accepted the proposition that merger analysis should concentrate considerably more on economic effects and a lot less on social and political effects.[10]

From a broader point of view, this trend in antitrust enforcement is unfortunate. And it is particularly so in the publishing world where the businessman's interest in selling information is inextricably intertwined with the public's interest in the free exchange of ideas. Whether or not the trend towards media concentration will have a deleterious effect on our society, however, is a matter that only time will tell.

PUBLISHERS' PRICING

On December 22, 1988, the Federal Trade Commission charged six major book publishers with illegally discriminating against independent bookstores by selling books at lower prices to major bookstore chains. The Commission thus inserted itself into a longstanding dispute between the dwindling number of independent bookstores and major book publishers by voting 3-to-1 to issue an administrative complaint against Harper & Row Publishers Inc., William Morrow and Co. and its owner The Hearst Corp., Macmillan Inc., The Putnam Berkley Group Inc., Random House Inc. and Simon & Schuster Inc.

The FTC complaint alleges that the six publishers violated the Robinson-Patman Act, which outlaws discrimination in prices between purchasers of commodities which has anti-competitive effects.[11] The complaint charges that the higher prices paid by the independent bookstores have limited their ability to compete with the nation's three largest bookstore chains—Crown Books Corp., owned by Washington's Haft family, B. Dalton Bookseller, and Waldenbooks Inc.—that allegedly received the lower prices.[12]

The publishers use pricing schedules in which the price is determined by the number of books in individual orders, according to the complaint, which was investigated by the FTC's Seattle Regional Office. On larger orders, purchasers pay a lower price per book than on smaller orders. The publishers allegedly treat orders placed by bookstore chains as a single order, even if the books are separately packed, itemized, and shipped to individual chain outlets. The chain stores allegedly pay lower prices than independent bookstores that receive shipments as large as or larger than the shipments to individual chain outlets.[13]

The case will initially be heard by an administrative law judge who will issue a finding after hearing arguments presented by the publishers and the commission staff. That decision can be appealed to the full commission. If the charges are upheld, the commission could order the publishers not to discriminate in price and to make all allowances, services, and facilities available on proportionately equal terms to all purchasers.[14]

The publishers would have a defense to the charge if they can prove that there was a "cost justification" for the price difference or that the lower prices were just the result of "meeting competition." In this case, the book publishers will not deny that they charge large retail chains less for their books than smaller, independent stores, but they claim that the cost difference accurately reflects the difference in selling and distributing books to independents versus chains.

The FTC claims that the chains enjoyed volume discounts to which they were not entitled. It cites evidence of orders placed by bookstore chains that were allegedly registered as a single purchase even though the books were separately packed, itemized, and shipped to individual chain outlets. Independent bookstores that received shipments as large or larger than individual chain outlets allegedly were forced to pay more for the same books.

The commission's chairman Daniel Oliver dissented from the FTC's action. He said that the price differences are probably justified because of the higher costs of selling to different stores as opposed to one chain. He added that the publishers' practices were probably designed to meet competition from other publishers. He also warned that an ultimate finding of liability may force publishers to adopt a more costly method for distribution that could lead to higher book prices.

The charges contained in the FTC complaint have been voiced by independent booksellers for years. Complaints were especially strong against the paperback book publishers and culminated in a lawsuit brought by the Northern California Booksellers Association (NCBA) several years ago. Although the court found that the lower costs of servicing the larger chains did not justify the lower prices that were charged to chains, the case was settled before any final ruling was issued.[15] As part of that settlement, the paperback publishers agreed to grant discounts to independent sellers who increase their sales year to year.[16]

In 1982, the NCBA brought suit against the Hearst Corporation, the parent of Avon Books, currently the eighth-largest publisher of mass market paperback books under the Robinson-Patman Act. The booksellers association charged that Avon had given "secret and preferential discounts" to Waldenbooks and B. Dalton Bookseller since the early 1970s and to Crown Books since 1978. The effect, the association said, was to give the chain stores a profit margin advantage that substantially enhanced their competitive position.

In 1986, the NCBA and Avon went to trial on the limited issue of whether Avon could prove its cost-justification defense. The two sides presented conflicting expert evidence analyzing the publisher's costs of doing business with the chains compared with the independents. The largest component of the publishers' costs, amounting to more than 75 percent of Avon's cost of selling to independents in northern California, was the maintenance of its sales force. And it was the expense of these sales representatives that the booksellers association most hotly challenged.

The NCBA argued that the sales representatives represent "a non-necessary cost" to many independents who do not wish to use their services. Many small stores do not stock certain categories of new titles and have a large selection of backlist titles that can be ordered through catalogues. In October 1986, U.S. District Judge Thelton E. Henderson agreed with the booksellers, calling the sales representatives "only marginally useful" to the booksellers in making purchasing decisions.[17]

Rejecting Avon's cost-justification defense, Judge Henderson said that Avon had no business records explaining why it originally granted a discount to the chain stores and that it did not formally put its policy for doing so in writing until nearly three years after the lawsuit was filed. Furthermore, he wrote, the secrecy of Avon's discount implies that it "did not have any objective criteria for granting discounts but did so in response to pressure from the chain stores."

In a finding strongly bolstering the booksellers' accusation that the chain-discounting policy had wide competitive impact, Judge Henderson found the evidence suggested that the extra revenue provided to the chains by the preferential discount helped the chains to increase the number of their retail outlets and to increase dramatically the volume of books purchased from Avon. As indicated above, the NCBA suit was eventually settled, but these issues will again be raised in the Federal Trade Commission action.

The impact that the FTC litigation may ultimately have on the publishing business is uncertain, of course. Even if the Government wins, it may not benefit the publishers' non-bookstore customers. Just as there were rumors for years that the chainstores were receiving better prices than the independent bookstores, so there are rumors that large libraries or universities receive lower prices than smaller institutions. Unfortunately for those smaller libraries, the Robinson-Patman Act appears to provide no protection to them.

In 1938, the Robinson-Patman Act was amended to include an exemption for non-profit institutions.[18] That amendment provides that "Nothing in [the Robinson-Patman Act] shall apply to purchases of their supplies for their own use by schools, colleges, universities, public libraries, churches, hospitals, and charitable institutions not operated for profit." This provision was added to allow vendors to be "charitable," if they wished, by giving lower prices to non-profit institutions than to commercial purchasers,[19] but it has the incidental effect of immunizing price discriminations *among* non-profit institutions.

CONCLUSION

As the world of publishing moves toward the Twenty-first Century, it is being racked with technological and financial change. Some of that change affects "competition" in the narrow sense that the word is used in the federal antitrust laws. To that extent, the courts may intervene to shape the direction of that change.

REFERENCES

1. David Aaron, *Agent of Influence* (1989).
2. New York Times, March 19, 1989, sec. 4, p. 7. col. 1. Others, such as J. Kendrick Noble, an analyst with Paine Webber in New York, "just don't believe that it's possible for a few giants to control the information flow around the world." Los Angeles Times, March 7, 1989, pt. 4, p. 1, col. 1.
3. Law books are not immune from the merger trend. Mead Corp., which operates the Lexis legal database, recently agreed to buy Michie Co., a legal publishing company, from Macmillan Inc. for $226.5 million. Wall Street Journal, Dec. 12, 1988, sec. 2, p. 6, col. 6.
4. The novelist George Garrett has recently written that the conglomerizing of book publishers "makes them unwieldy and inefficient," making it "harder and harder to turn a profit with anything even slightly more demanding than the works of Bill Cosby or the meditations of Michael Jackson." Chicago Tribune, Jan. 2, 1989, Tempo, p. 2.
5. Wash. Post, Nov. 27, 1988, p. Hl. According to Bagdikian, about 55 percent of the book industry's revenue is controlled by about six of the 2,500 publishers based in the United States; six magazine publishing companies (among 11,000 in this country) control half that industry. The newspaper business is slightly more diverse, with about 12 companies controlling 50 percent of total national circulation.

6. American Banker, Dec. 5, 1988, p. 4.
7. *See Standard Oil Co. v. F.T.C.*, 340 U.S. 231, 249 (1951).
8. 15 U.S.C. §18.
9. *See generally Brown Shoe Co. v. United States*, 370 U.S. 294, 311-23 (1962) (emphasizing, among other things, that Congress wanted to protect small business).
10. *See, e.g.*, Department of Justice Merger Guidelines (released June 14, 1984). In contrast to Congress' earlier concerns about increasing concentration, the Reagan Administration viewed merger activity positively. The Guidelines state, for example:

> Although they sometimes harm competition, mergers generally play an important role in a free enterprise economy. They can penalize ineffective management and facilitate the efficient flow of investment capital and the redeployment of existing productive assets. While challenging competitively harmful mergers, the Department seeks to avoid unnecessary interference with that larger universe of mergers that are either competitively beneficial or neutral.

11. Section 2(a) of the Clayton Act (15 U.S.C. §13), popularly known as the Robinson-Patman Act, prohibits sellers from discriminating in price among different purchasers of commodities of like grade and quality where the effect may be to injure competition. The seller may be able to justify the price discrimination under one or more of the following defenses set forth in the Act: cost justification (Section 2(a)); changing conditions (*id.*); or meeting competition (Section 2(b)).
12. The use of the Robinson-Patman Act in connection with chainstore discounts is historically appropriate. At the time the Robinson-Patman Act was enacted in 1936, product distribution systems in the United States had been in a state of significant transformation since before the beginning of the twentieth century. Through the use of multiple outlets and the vertical integration of the wholesale and retail functions, chain store entrepreneurs (such as A&P) consolidated their purchases so as to make maximum use of quantity and similar discounts from suppliers. The Great Depression caused independent retailers, particularly in the grocery and drug industries, to suffer severe economic hardship, and much of this hardship was traced to the chains. The independents carried their complaints to Congress with the result that a number of anti-chain legislative efforts were undertaken. These culminated in the Robinson-Patman Act.
13. In addition, the complaints allege that some or all of the publishers have granted favored customers additional discounts not shown on published pricing schedules and have provided chains with special services or facilities for promotion and inventory control.
14. In addition, under Section 5(a) of the Clayton Act (15 U.S.C. §16(a)), private litigants may use a final judgment or decree "rendered in any civil or criminal proceeding brought by . . . the United States under the antitrust laws to the effect that a defendant has violated said laws shall be prima facie evidence against such defendant in any action or proceeding brought by any other party

against such defendant. . . ." Several courts have held that an FTC order or judgment is one "under the antitrust laws" to trigger §5(a) when the commission enforces the Clayton Act. *E.g., Purex Corp. v. Proctor & Gamble Co.*, 453 F.2d 288 (9th Cir. 1971), cert. denied, 405 U.S. 1065 (1972).

15. *See* The New York Times, Mar. 17, 1987, Sec. D at 1, col. 3.

16. Since that lawsuit, and particularly in recent months, paperback publishers have significantly improved their pricing policies, according to Andy Ross, owner of Cody's Books, an independent bookstore in Berkeley, Calif., and a member of American Booksellers Association's board of directors. *See* The Washington Post, Dec. 23, 1988, page D1. Ross said, however, that the booksellers welcome the FTC action, particularly because independent booksellers have no way of monitoring the issue of "under the table" arrangements, such as unpublished discounts and promotional allowances, which the FTC has said it will tackle. *Id.*

17. *See* The New York Times, Mar. 17, 1987, Sec. D at 1, col. 3.

18. May 26, 1938, c. 283, 52 Stat. 446, 15 U.S.C. §13c.

19. *Cf. Abbott Laboratories v. Portland Retail Druggists Assn., Inc.*, 425 U.S. 1 (1976); *Logan Lanes, Inc. v. Brunswick Corp.*, 378 F.2d 212 (9th Cir. 1967), cert. denied, 389 U.S. 898.

Acquisitions and the FTC:
A Brief Introduction

Suzanne Krebsbach

SUMMARY. Because acquisitions librarians deal in large part with publishers and vendors, librarians should be familiar with laws regulating the publishing industry. Commercial practices in general are regulated by the Federal Trade Commission which issues industry guides for the governing of various industries or practices. The American Library Association and the American Association of Law Libraries have long-established committees that moderate relations between libraries and publishers.

When dealing with publishers and vendors, the acquisition librarian should be aware of Federal laws governing the publishing industry. The Federal Trade Commission was established in 1915 as an independent administrative organization to regulate trade. Its principal functions are to promote commerce through the prevention of general trade restraints such as price-fixing agreements, boycotts, illegal combinations of competitors and other unfair methods of competition. The Commission safeguards the public by proscribing false or deceptive advertisement, and discrimination in pricing. The Commission enforces the laws by promoting voluntary compliance and litigation in Federal courts. Cases are instituted by registering a complaint, and can be settled by consent orders.

Anyone — consumers, librarians, or competitors — can file a complaint with the Commission. Generally, a letter giving the facts in detail is sufficient to initiate proceedings, but the letter should be accompanied by all available evidence to support the charge. When

Suzanne Krebsbach is Librarian and Records Manager at the McNair Law Firm, in Columbia, SC.

a complaint is received staff attorneys determine if an investigation is warranted to achieve the Commission's goal of maintaining competition and protecting comsumers.

For example, in 1988 the Federal Trade Commission charged six of the nation's largest book publishers, Harper & Row, Macmillan, Hearst, Simon & Schuster, Random House, and Putnam, Berkely, with illegally discriminating against independent bookstores by selling books at lower prices to major bookstore chains, in violation of the Robinson-Patman Act. The complainants allege that, through discriminatory pricing practices, the publishers sell or distribute books at lower prices to some retailers ("favored purchasers") than to other retailers ("disfavored purchasers"). The favored purchasers allegedly include the nation's three largest bookstore chains, Waldenbooks, B. Dalton Booksellers, and Crown Books. The disfavored purchasers allegedly include most, if not all, of the nation's independent bookstores.

If the charges are upheld, the Commission could order the publishers not to discriminate in price and to make all allowances, services, and facilities available on proportionally equal terms to all purchasers. Commission Chairman Daniel Oliver opposed the charge. He believed issuance of a complaint was not in the public interest, because the litigation process and an ultimate finding of liability may force publishers to adopt less efficient distribution methods and thereby lead to higher book prices for consumers.[1]

In addition to regulating discriminatory pricing and other matters, the Commission issues industry-specific guides and trade practice rules. Such guides are not law, but are the Commission's interpretation of the laws it administers. This is for the guidance of the public in conducting its affairs in conformity with legal requirements. The guides provide the basis for voluntary, simultaneous abandonment of unlawful practices by members of an industry and may relate to a practice common to many industries or to specific practices of a particular industry.[2] Failure to comply with the guides may result in corrective action by the Commission under applicable statutory provisions. The Commission has, for example, developed guides for a number of industries such as manufacturers of metallic watchbands, mirrors, and hosiery, as well as guides concerning the use of the word "free" and similar representations in advertising.

The publishing industry as a whole has not generated substantial complaints. However, librarians should be aware of several trade-related commission guides, specifically the guide for law book industry.[3] In this guide the Commission has defined the terms treatise, set (of books), series, and loose-leaf binder. The guide carefully describes regulations concerning new revisions or replacement sets or series as well as defining the terms "new," "current," or "up-to-date" in relation to books. The guide addresses disclosure of proper titles of texts and treatises, and representations of works not yet published.

> Solicitations relative to works not yet published should clearly and conspicuously disclose that the publication is being planned or contemplated and that inquiries or orders are being solicited to determine demand for the publication, or words to that effect.[4]

The guide also devotes a lengthy section to disclosures on publications. Publishers are instructed to disclose clearly and conspicuously, on the title page, half-title page and/or verso, the full title of the book, including any subtitles. There must be clear and unambiguous identification of authors, editors or compilers, as well as the city and state of publication.[5]

The guide devotes an entire section to regulating billing practices. Among other things, publishers have the responsibility of applying all correspondence and payments to the correct account, and where there is any question, notifying the customer before entering the pertinent data into the computer system. Approval items must be clearly and separately identified. All invoices must show a clear and readable description of each item. If abbreviations are used which are not readily understandable, the invoice should have attached to it a clear interpretation. The guide, in this section, describes the basic information which should be provided for the billing process. This section does not relieve the publisher of his responsibility to comply with Fair Credit Billing Act (15 *U.S.C.* section 1601), and law book sellers should note in particular section 161 of that Act dealing with "Correction of Billing Errors."[6]

In general, the guide declares that no publication should be advertised, published, or otherwise represented in any manner which may mislead or deceive purchasers of the grade, quality. material, size, contents, authorship, editorship, use, value, price, origin, preparation, manufacture, or date of publication or copyright of any publication.[7] In addition, the adding of volumes or other materials, the overall content of which is not substantially germane to the subject of the basic work, constitutes an unfair trade practice.[8] Unfair trade practices are also actionable under state law in many states. In South Carolina, for example, one has recourse to the "Unfair Trade Practices Act" (*S.C. Code*, section 39-5-10 et seq.). State laws permit additional course of action to consumers.

In order to carry out the mission of preventing unfair commercial practices, the Federal Trade Commission relies on "voluntary and cooperative" procedures. Through these means the Commission provides authoritative guidance to businesses and industry. The Commission will issue an advisory opinion when asked to determine the outcome of a proposed action or commercial policy. Such opinions are binding, but the Commission may reconsider if the public input seems to justify it.[9]

The library profession has long been interested in the unique relationship with the publishing industry. In 1961 the American Library Association established a Fair Trade Practices Committee which later became the Bookdealer/Library Relations Committee of the Resources and Technical Services Division. In 1986 the committee became a division committee with the name Publisher/Vendor-Library Relations Committee. The essential mission of this group is

> to serve as the review and advisory committee on all matters of vendors of library materials-library relationships; to investigate these relationships; and to prepare recommendations and develop guidelines of acceptable performance for libraries and vendors for ordering and supplying library materials.[10]

The committee is composed of seven regular members as well as consultants, interns, and liaisons. The membership is balanced between librarians and publishers/vendors, providing a valuable exchange between members of the industry and the library profession. This committee meets at the ALA midwinter meeting and at the annual summer conference. At these occasions the committee reports to the membership in an open forum. In 1987-1988 the committee handled less than a dozen complaints and requests for information. In the absence of major issues, the committee focused on problems in serial pricing.

The American Association of Law Libraries has a similar group called Committee on Relations with Information Vendors which deals with problems of electronic publishing as well as traditional publishing. This committee, when it was formed over twenty years ago, was known as the Committee on Relations with Publishers and Dealers. Its function is analogous to that of the ALA committee: to facilitate communication between librarians and members of the publishing industry in a cooperative working relationship.

If one has a problem with a publisher or vendor, the first step in resolving the problem is discussing it with the representative, if there is one. Publisher/vendor representatives are an important link between the library consumer and the industry producer. From an industry point of view, it is critical to respond to consumer's concerns, because the business depends on it. If one is unable to resolve a problem after discussion with the representative, then one should contact the ALA or AALL committee, which will assist both parties in reaching an agreement.

REFERENCES

1. CCH *Trade Regulation Reports*, paragraph 22,634.
2. 16 *Code of Federal Regulation* 256; hereinafter cited as CFR.
3. 16 *CFR* 256, et seq.
4. 16 *CFR* 256.7
5. 16 *CFR* 256.11
6. 16 *CFR* 256.5
7. 16 *CFR* 256.17
8. 16 *CFR* 256.16
9. *The U.S. Government Manual* (Washington: GPO, 1987-1988). p. 573.
10. Margaret Maes Axtman, "Publishers/Vendors—Library Relations Committee," *American Association of Law Libraries Newsletter* 20:7, pp 11-12. See also Margaret Maes Axtmann, "Publishers Advertising: a Legitimate Complaint," *Library Acquisitions: Practice and Theory* 10:pp 113-116.

Publisher Advertising:
Proposal for a New Era

Margaret Maes Axtmann

SUMMARY. This essay describes legal and ethical aspects of publisher advertising and offers considerations for change.

In the business of library acquisitions publisher/vendor relations has received increasing attention in the literature, at professional meetings, and in the operations of acquisitions departments of all types and sizes. Typically the focus of this attention is on pricing, order fulfillment, reporting and other services offered by the book industry. It seems odd that the publisher relations movement in the general library world has failed to focus on a glaring weakness in most publishing houses, one which causes emotions ranging from irritation to anguish among acquisitions librarians and bibliographers. That weakness is in the quality of publisher advertising.

The labor-intensive aspects of technical services in a library require managers to search continually for time-saving methods. In acquisitions departments, where ordering and receiving are a race against the clock, quantifying the steps that lead to the placement of an order is dependent on the quality of the information available to the searcher. A minimum number of bibliographic elements must be present in order to make the job easier: author, title, full imprint, date of publication and edition. Reprint or series information, number of volumes, publication schedules for multi-volume works, price and available discount plans are additional essential elements that assist in making an intelligent choice of vendor. Rarely does

Margaret Maes Axtmann is Acquisitions Librarian/Foreign and International Law Bibliographer, for Cornell Law Library, Myron Taylor Hall, Ithaca, NY 14853-4901.

21

advertising from general publishers have all these elements, yet they are vital to the selection, pre-order searching and acquisitions processes.

LEGAL ISSUES

For law librarians the issue of publisher advertising is not a new one. Twenty years ago, an article by Raymond Taylor entitled "Lawbook Consumers Need Protection"[1] was the impetus for an investigation by the Federal Trade Commission (FTC) into the practices of the law book industry. Among the practices cited by Taylor as objectionable were several pertaining to misleading or incomplete advertising. Major complaints included advertisements that appeared to be invoices, listing of titles without publication dates, labeling a publication as new when it was really more than two years old, representing a publication as a monograph when it was part of a larger set, and failing to include prices on advertisements. Groups such as the American Bar Association, the American Association of Law Libraries and the American Bar Foundation actively studied the problem. In 1975 the Federal Trade Commission promulgated the *Guides for the Law Book Industry*,[2] which became effective on April 8, 1976. Such industry guides are administrative interpretations of laws administered by the Commission for the guidance of the public in conducting its affairs in conformity with legal requirements.[3]

Because the FTC guidelines pertain to law books and other materials designed for use primarily by the legal community, they are important to acquisitions librarians and collection development specialists in law libraries of all types. Few academic and public librarians are aware of them, however, even though legal materials are purchased in many general libraries. It is unfortunate that it was necessary to regulate the practices of an industry that could not regulate itself, but, now that the guidelines exist, few law publishers knowingly violate them in their advertising and marketing practices. Among the disclosures that are mandated for both direct-mail advertising and oral presentations by sales representatives are name and address of the publisher, full title of the work, author, copyright date and whether supplemented, whether it is part of a set or a series, a description of the subject matter, type of binding and price.[4] Federal law regarding false or deceptive advertising exists in Title 15 of the United States Code[5] and is administered by the Federal Trade Commission, an independent administrative agency created by statute.[6] It is under this framework that the *Guides for the Law Book Industry* were proposed and promulgated. Unfortunately, although numerous violations of the FTC guidelines have been reported to the FTC since 1976, a representative of the FTC has stated in public that the guidelines have worked well and there have been few complaints recorded.[7] It also is interesting to note that in two recent publications, one on advertising compliance[8] and one a legal guide for book publishers,[9] the issue of publisher advertising is totally ignored. Plevan and Siroky discuss industry guides for specific products but do not mention those for law books.[10] Clearly regulation is not the entire solution to the problem.

ETHICAL ISSUES

Why don't similar requirements exist for the entire industry? The astonishing answer is that they do, at least in part. In 1979 the American National Standards Institute published Z39.13, the American National Standard for Describing Books in Advertisements, Catalogs, Promotional Materials, and Book Jackets.[11] The astonishment lies in the fact that few librarians or publishers seem aware that such a standard exists, in spite of the wide publicity that Z39 standards normally generate. Z39.13 defines ten types of promotional media and four different markets to which promotional material is addressed. For each defined category of promotional material, the recommended bibliographic elements to be included on advertising to the various markets are listed. The information is presented in textual as well as tabular form, and the coverage is reasonably comprehensive.

Z39.13 was reaffirmed without change in 1984, and balloting for reaffirmation in 1989 has just closed, with the results not yet public. Are publishers and librarians satisfied with the standard, or is it even understood by the voting organizations? It is not a standard that needs substantial revision; rather it needs to be expanded to include serials, microforms, media, computer files and other formats. Above all, it needs greater publicity and wider distribution to librarians and publishers alike. The standard is meant to provide guidance, and compliance is entirely voluntary. The lengthy and expensive process of establishing a Z39 standard should affirm its importance, however, and anything less than an honest attempt at full compliance is unconscionable.

In spite of this list of laws, regulations and standards, this problem could be controlled by the industry itself. Just as publishers have listened to the needs of librarians in many other areas, it is likely that they would be ready to hear criticism of their promotional materials and take steps to change them. Library/publisher relations need not, indeed should not, be adversarial.

An ethical approach by librarians is one which carefully describes the need for complete and accurate information to be on every piece of publisher advertising. Rather than finding faster and better ways to seek out missing bibliographic elements, librarians should ask publishers to supply the information from their own sources. From both a business and an ethical point of view, the response cannot be anything but receptive and compliant. Publishers should acknowledge the needs of librarians by incorporating into all advertising the elements necessary to make intelligent selection and acquisitions decisions. These include author, title, imprint, date of publication, reprint information, relationship to other sets or series, subject matter, intended audience, type of binding and price. All information should be clearly stated in a prominent place on the advertisement. Sales representatives, including telemarketing staff, should be able to provide all of these elements if asked. Additionally publishers should not resort to using advertisements that resemble invoices or renewal forms. Nor should they represent a work as having been published if it has in fact not been written or is not yet published.

CONCLUSION

A new era of publisher advertising is one in which the content and quality of promotional material is regulated by the publishing industry itself. Librarians and publishers should work together to achieve the highest standard of advertising information for all types of published material. The needs of collection development and acquisitions staff in a variety of libraries must be taken into consideration if such a standard is to be realized. While the direct cost of materials purchased by libraries remains an issue of great concern to the library world, the hidden costs of dealing with inadequate information must not be overlooked. This essay challenges librarians and publishers to begin the new era now with a cooperative venture designed to improve the quality of publisher advertising.

REFERENCES

1. Taylor, "Lawbook Consumers Need Protection," 55 *A.B.A. J.* 553 (1969).
2. *Guides for the Law Book Industry*, 40 Fed. Reg. 33,436 (1975), codified at 16 C.F.R. §256 (1988).
3. 16 C.F.R. §1.5 (1988).
4. 16 C.F.R. §256.1 (1988). For further information about the history and provisions of the *Guides* see Axtmann, Publisher Advertising: A Legitimate Complaint, 10 *Library Acquisitions: Practice and Theory* 113 (1986) and Kosek, Law Librarians as Consumer Advocates, 9 *Publications Clearing House Bull.* 26 (1986).
5. Lanham Act §43(a), 15 U.S.C. §1125 (1982), amended by Act of Nov. 16, 1988, Pub. L. No. 100-667 (effective Nov. 16, 1989).
6. 16 C.F.R. §0.1 (1988).
7. Statement by Lewis Franke, panel discussion titled "The FTC Guides for the Law Book Industry: Have They Worked?" at the 79th Annual Meeting of the American Association of Law Libraries, July 9, 1986. Reported at 9 *Publications Clearing House Bull.* 88 (1986).
8. Plevan, Kenneth A. and Siroky, Miriam L. *Advertising Compliance Handbook*. New York: Practising Law Institute, 1988.
9. Duboff, Leonard D. *Book Publishers' Legal Guide*. Seattle: Butterworth Legal Publishers, 1984.
10. Plevan and Siroky, *op. cit.*, 188-198.
11. American National Standards Institute, *American National Standard for Describing Books in Advertisements, Catalogs, Promotional Materials, and Book Jackets* (1979). Reaffirmed by ballot in 1984 and now published by the National Information Standards Organization.

Plain English for Publishers:
An Articulation of Billing Problems

Marcie Stevenson Kingsley
Philip C. Berwick

SUMMARY. Billing practices of publishers are among the points of continued discussion between librarians and publishers' representatives. While many means are available for communication, cooperation, and problem resolution between these groups, significant problems such as incomprehensible invoices, billing for supplements only marginally related to current subscriptions, and renewal notices sent to non-subscribing libraries continue. These are practices of relatively few — but some very prolific — publishers. This situation is true even in the law book industry despite the existence of detailed Federal Trade Commission guidelines regulating legal publishing and despite the interdependence of the major publishers of legal materials and their consumers. Neither federal regulations nor the concepts of fairness and goodwill have eliminated these problems. Some modest proposals are included.

Would your library pay $432 for the following?

MFP-MARCH 1989 REV W/TOP COVER VOL IAPT2
R#81 & MARCH 89 CUM SP & REV/V8-8C R#44

Or perhaps $238.60 for the material listed below?

HORWITZ FEB89 REV/V1-1C & STAR VOLS R# 40 & 89
REV/V2-4 W/TOP COVER V3 R#60

A large publishing company regularly sends invoices for standing orders that are as confusing as those quoted above; in addition, print

---

Marcie Stevenson Kingsley is Head of Technical Services and Philip C. Berwick is Director of the Library at George Mason University Law Library, 3401 North Fairfax Drive, Arlington, VA 22201.

quality of the bills is so poor that legibility is frequently marginal —
that may be "Horvitz" or "Hurwitz" on the original of the second
bill above — and trying to make readable photocopies for local record keeping is sometimes useless.

Perhaps the publisher has very good reasons for these poor quality bills; certainly librarians have learned through dialogue with
publishers and with vendors that it is vital to try to understand the
viewpoint of the publisher or other seller. Yet why is it that hun-
dreds of publishers can manage to send invoices that are clear and
understandable? And how is it that some companies can even issue
an invoice that is self-explanatory, legible, available in triplicate,
and includes the former title of the subscription being billed?

Another common invoice problem is bibliographic identification.
The bill may have only an approximation of the title, e.g., *Corporate Public Affairs*, when the actual title of the volume is *National
Directory of Corporate Public Affairs*. Then there are the subscription invoices received for such things as "Federal Taxes Library,"
a phrase which does not necessarily correspond to the title of any
subscription but rather to a group of four or five subscriptions that
the library receives and checks in under their respective titles.

A minor but maddening problem is poor physical format. Some
invoices come in minute sizes such as seven and one-half by three
and one-half inches. These bills always seem to be from the publishers that cannot supply multiple-copy forms, so these diminutive
slips of paper are at great risk of being lost somewhere along the
paper trail.

Of course a great annoyance to librarians is the infamous non-
invoice. These are the missives that list the library's name, address,
account number, a title, and the price; a library staff member not
well-acquainted with non-invoices may spend considerable time
trying to verify the need for payment before noticing the words
"This is not an invoice. This is a solicitation." (Donald Dunn, Law
Librarian at Western New England College of Law, suggests that
libraries send to offending publishers printed forms that look like
purchase orders but which carry the note, "THIS IS NOT AN OR-
DER; IT IS A REQUEST FOR A FREE BOOK.")[1]

It is also the bills for material not ordered, bills for subscriptions
that have been canceled several times over, and bills for supplements only casually related to a series on order, but automatically

shipped and invoiced, that raise the ire of librarians. Then there are the multi-part series which split into yet more series, again automatically shipped, to be followed at the next renewal date by a price increase clearly more substantial than necessary to cover the cost of the new sub-series.

A large majority of the above problems arise from a small number of publishers; most of this group act as sole distributors for their material rather than dealing through vendors. (Some publishers who continue these practices are somewhat willing to sell through jobbers but find themselves no less unpopular with jobbers than they are with librarians.) while librarians can usually change vendors if service is not satisfactory, they have no choice but to deal directly with the sole distributors to get the published products they need no matter how poor the service.

LIBRARIAN-PUBLISHER COMMUNICATIONS

If vendors or jobbers cannot be the solution to problem billings in many cases, what other options exist? For one thing, opportunities abound for librarians and publishers to share their views. Billing practices and many other issues such as distribution methods, accelerated journal price increases, discriminatory or differential foreign subscription pricing, less-than-forthright advertising practices, issuing one publication under two different names (or in only slightly differing forms), and numerous other ethical and legal questions have provided publishers and librarians with more than enough to discuss through the rapidly developing modes of communication that have become so important to acquisitions personnel.

The library science literature has provided a ready platform for advocating greater attentiveness from publishers to librarians' complaints about publishers' practices. Library science journals and newsletters carry articles frankly expressing dissatisfaction with aspects of the publishing universe. Anecdotes about and analyses of annoying or legally questionable practices appear regularly in the library press.[2] This one-way communication may or may not be very effective in changing the behavior of the publishers in question, but it certainly provides valuable warnings to library colleagues. (To date, it does not appear that publishers have risked commenting so openly on library practices or on individual libraries in, for example, the pages of *Publishers Weekly*.)

Professional meetings have come to play a large role in providing opportunities for discussion and occasions for problem-resolution among librarians, publishers, and vendors. The obvious willingness of vendors' representatives to participate actively has assured a greater level of cooperation with librarians than is apparent in the publisher-librarian relationship. Lively discussions do take place among all three groups, however, at the open meetings of the Publisher/Vendor-Library Relations Committee of the Resources and Technical Services Division at ALA annual and mid-winter conferences; these sessions have been excellent chances for librarians, publishers, and vendors to learn about each other's likes, dislikes, and modes of operation. Similarly, the American Association of Publishers/Resources and Technical Services Division Joint Committee has provided forums for mutually working out problems and sharing information related to topics such as out-of-print material and serials marketing. The North American Serials Interest Group and the Issues in Book and Serials Acquisitions Charleston Conferences have been born and have flourished in the last decade because of the interaction among the several sectors of the information enterprise.

Areas of discussion have naturally followed the development of electronic publishing as noted in an article by Karen Hunter in *Journal of Library Administration*.[3] Another recent development is the creation of small advisory groups and focus groups in which librarians can readily give input to publishers on products, publication needs, and marketing; though for a few companies focus groups have long been a way of doing business, for most companies involved the groups are new institutions.[4] Another recent noteworthy event was the extensive American Association of Publishers/Resources and Technical Services Division survey of the library market completed in 1987; this was a major attempt to update information (not collected and analyzed on such a large scale since a similar joint survey in the mid-1970's) about the purchasing habits and preferences of the complex library market.[5]

With all these opportunities for communication, it would seem that librarians' complaints would be heard. Of course there have been many successes, but the problems delineated above continue with definite consistency.

WHEN DISCUSSION FAILS, POLICING MAY HELP

Some of the interaction between publishers and librarians is based much less on sharing information than on resolving rather serious disputes. Corrective action is an important phase of the work of ALA's RTSD Publisher/Vendor-Library Relations Committee mentioned above. The committee carries on considerable correspondence about publishing practices, hears complaints, and meets in closed session at ALA conferences. The American Association of Law Libraries' Committee on Relations with Information Vendors also provides an extensive process for dealing with librarians' complaints about the law-materials publishing industry, particularly as related to the Federal Trade Commission's "Guides for the Law Book Industry," part of the *Code of Federal Regulations*.[6] Though not compulsory, these guidelines combined with the continuing vigilance of law librarians have brought about substantial cooperation from some responsible publishers.

A close look at the well-organized approach of law librarians to publishing concerns is instructive. In the law book publishing industry, there are a few major publishers who produce a considerable volume of key materials. Most of these publishers are sole distributors. Without vendors to perform as what Edward Lockman describes as buffers or shock absorbers,[7] substantial irritation will probably continue to exist between librarians and publishers of legal materials. However, the situation is clearly better than it was in the late 1960's when dissatisfaction with distribution practices, issuance of so-called new editions with very little new information, and piggybacking of expensive supplementation onto basic subscriptions led to impressive activism by librarians.

Actions leading up to publication of the FTC "Guides for the Law Book Industry" are a fascinating chapter in American library history. An influential article by then North Carolina Supreme Court Librarian Raymond Taylor in the *American Bar Association Journal* in 1969 and a related analysis by Julius Marke in *Law Library Journal* the following year provide insight into the practices that had long strained the relationships between the producers and the consumers of legal material.[8] The American Association of Law Libraries initiated and has maintained a structured approach to communicating librarians' complaints to publishers, vendors, and the FTC. The Committee on Relations with Information Vendors, formerly the Committee on Relations with Publishers and Dealers, makes complaint-reporting forms readily available and summarizes recent complaints (as well as the explanations received from publishers and vendors and descriptions of resolution of problems) in issues of the newsletter *The CRIV Sheet*.

This newsletter is now being included in the mailing of the general newsletter of the Association, so every member of the American Association of Law Libraries gets to see the offensive deeds described. This means that not only acquisitions and serials librarians in law libraries are reading the names of the problem publishers: so are collection development, catalog, and reference librarians and library directors.

THE RESULTS OF COMMUNICATION AND POLICING

How effective have all these means of interaction between librarians and publishers been in bringing about changes in practices? There are still a number of publishers the mention of whose very names bring anguished looks to the faces of librarians. Even in the law book and serial industry, where publishing is most carefully covered by FTC guidelines and where publishers must depend on a relatively narrow community for consumption of their publications, the problems are chronic. Most of the problems and annoyances cited throughout this article were provided compliments of law publishers. The unintelligible invoices quoted on the first page of this article came from a major legal publisher, though 16 CFR 256.15 prescribes billing practices:

> All industry product invoices should show . . . 2) a clear and readable description of each item or unit. If abbreviations are used which are not readily understandable, the invoice should have thereon or attached thereto a clear interpretation of said abbreviations;

Again, even if the publisher of MFP-MARCH 1989 REV/V1-1C & STAR VOLS R#40 & 89 REV/V2-4 W/TOP COVER V3 R#60 has an excellent explanation of why invoices must read this way, alas, how is it that some companies can provide invoices with easy-to-read lists of abbreviations on the reverse?

No, all the billing and related problems have not been solved. At least two publishers of legal materials repeatedly send invoices for subscriptions and standing orders canceled years ago—though 16 CFR 256.10 states that subscription renewals should not be sent to a person, firm, library, or entity not currently subscribing. It happens that these same two publishers, however, will begin NEW subscriptions with amazing ease—just a call to the sales representative, and the new series is on its way.

In addition, there are two legal publishers that issue one- and two-volume monographs which are updated once or twice a year with paperbound supplements; general academic and public libraries as well as law libraries purchase these titles, but not all libraries want to use the updating services. The updates arrive anyway, unordered, accompanied by a bill. The voices responding at the 800 numbers for these companies may persuade a librarian that the update is so vital to use of the monograph that no library—at least no self-respecting library—has ever chosen not to be on standing order for the supplements. In reality, however, even very good libraries may choose not to purchase every update.

PERSPECTIVE

The kinds of problems cited must indeed appear minor to companies whose legal concerns involve major actions such as company mergers, defending against lawsuits, negotiating book contracts, and handling copyright matters.

Except for a relatively few publishers, libraries are not the major source of income. Estimates of the proportion of publishing industry sales to libraries vary, and figures are most readily available for trade and professional books, which do not reflect the entire publishing structure.[9] The percentage is not large, however, and, as one author has noted, a segment of the market that spends a relatively small percentage cannot expect to call the shots.[10] Veteran bookman Edward Lockman wrote, "I cannot remember the last time a publisher designed or altered his or her operational procedures for the sole intention of library convenience."[11] Thus we find that even in the law book publishing industry, where law libraries are a major market for the expensive looseleaf publications and multi-part serials, the disgrace of being cited time and again in the pages of their customers' major newsletter is not enough to change some everyday practices.

PROPOSALS

It is necessary for librarians to set forth requirements strongly and in the same plain English that must be forthcoming from publishers. The FTC "Guides for the Law Book Industry" quoted in part do set forth definite criteria which should result in clearer invoices. Although these guides are not compulsory, they should be taken seriously by publishers and should be considered the minimum requirements for invoice clarity. Certainly no seller should be providing invoices which have to be translated or, even worse, deciphered. And any pleading by a publisher that nonsensical invoices are due to an antiquated invoicing system or short fixed field lengths requiring sharply truncated titles is simply not acceptable. If an invoice is not clear (as determined by a librarian), it does not deserve to be paid until it is clarified by the publisher.

It is not unreasonable to require the courtesy of a publishing company responding with a written clarification — in plain English — for the second invoice example on page one of this article ("Horwitz") so that it reads

> *Patent Office Rules and Practice*, Horwitz
> Feb. 89 revision for vols. 1-1C: supplements
> Feb. 89 release #40 for vols. labeled "*": loose-leaf filings
> 1989 annual revision for vols. 2-4: supplements plus replacement binders (top covers only)
> Feb. 89 release #60 for vol. 3

If certain publishers continue failing to comply with librarians' insistence on knowing what they are being asked to pay for and on being billed only for material ordered, the profession may have to give them more help. Some vague language in the FTC Guides may need to be supplemented by examples provided by librarians. The criteria may need to spell out "Invoices should look like this . . ." Librarians, through their professional associations, are appropriate authorities to look at the FTC guidelines, to propose amplification, and to consider whether similar definitions are needed to apply specifically to all the segments of the publishing industry not covered by the "Guides for the Law Book Industry."

Law librarians have obviously tried in a number of ways to influence the format of the information found in publishers' invoices. Turning to the federal government for assistance has helped somewhat; FTC Guides were promulgated to cover a variety of law publishing practices. However, because of the voluntary nature of the guides, no sanctions resulted for non-compliance. Informal discussions and professional meetings have served as other routes toward cooperation with all areas of the publishing industry; grievances have been aired individually and collectively.

While it is true that composing a set of criteria for law publishers has had a salutary effect on some, it is also true that others have still not seen fit to adjust their billing and related distribution practices to meet the criteria set forth in the regulation. It is time to complete the work begun by the FTC Guides by insisting that the criteria set down in them become the standard used by publishers. This will require a more activist approach by librarians but will be precious time well spent. The results will be a more efficient billing system than now exists and library collections that are up to date while lacking redundant, unordered material.

REFERENCES

1. Donald J. Dunn, letter to the Editor, *The CRIV Sheet: Newsletter of the Committee on Relations with Information Vendors* (American Association of Law Libraries) 11, no. 2 (November, 1988): 2.

2. Henry M. Yaple, "People in Hell Want Ice Water, Too," *Library Acquisitions: Practice & Theory* 11, no. 3 (1987): 223-226.

Recent issues of *The CRIV Sheet* and its predecessor *Publications Clearing House Bulletin*.

3. Karen Hunter, "Academic Librarians and Publishers: Customers versus

Producers or Partners in the Planning of Electronic Publishing?" *Journal of Library Administration* 9, no. 4 (1988): 35-47.

4. Robert Burroughs, "Book Publishers Focus on Librarian Focus Groups," *Library Journal* 114, no. 5 (March 15, 1989): 48-49.

5. Hendrik Edelman and Karen Muller, "A New Look at the Library Market," *Publishers Weekly* 231, no. 21 (May 29, 1987): 30-35.

J. Fletcher, "Examining the Library Market," *Publishers Weekly* 232 (August 14, 1987): 15.

6. 16 CFR 256 (1988).

7. Edward J. Lockman, "Is the Customer Always Right; Or Wait a Minute, Don't You Want My Business?" *Library Acquisitions: Practice & Theory* 11, no. 2 (1987): 121-123.

8. Raymond M. Taylor, "Law Book Consumers Need Protection," *American Bar Association Journal* 55 (1969): 553-556.

Julius J. Marke, "The Gentle Art of Making Enemies or Law Book Publishing Revisited," *Law Library Journal* 63 (1970): 3-13.

9. "Consumer Book Sales in Healthy Uptrend," *Standard and Poor's Industry Surveys* (November, 1988, looseleaf edition): M39-M40 ("Libraries account for about 13% of the total dollar value of publishers' book sales and about 5% of units sold in any given year," p. M40).

10. Wanda Dole, "Librarians, Publishers, and Vendors: Looking for Mr. Goodbuy," *Library Acquisitions: Practice and Theory* 11, no. 2 (1987): 128.

11. Edward J. Lockman, "Is the Customer Always Right," p. 122.

The Library Perspective
on Non-Cash Charitable Contributions

Corrie Marsh

SUMMARY. The donor of a charitable gift of non-cash property is entitled to an income tax deduction if the donor complies with Internal Revenue Service regulations. As the recipients of gift contributions of books, manuscripts, paintings, and art objects, libraries are obligated to maintain records of these gifts and provide donor information. Many libraries are finding it difficult to keep informed about the gift tax law changes during 1984-88. The intent of this paper is to review the legislative changes since 1982 and delineate current regulations. Although the author is not a tax or legal authority, her experience with practical records maintenance for non-cash gifts is offered as guidance for libraries wishing to expand their gift operations or review their current policies.

BACKGROUND

The 1980's have been a changing environment for organizations that depend on non-cash gift contributions. Libraries have traditionally strengthened their collections with gifts of private libraries, manuscripts, books, paintings, art objects and other forms of materials. By 1982, donors of property donations were permitted to claim an income tax deduction without itemizing their tax returns. It is presumed that many donors claimed full market value or purchase price for these gifts, while some donors of art claimed deductions in excess of fair market value. In any event, with the Tax Reform Act of 1984, the Internal Revenue Service enforced increased control over the valuation of non-cash gifts with requirements for certified

Corrie Marsh is Acquisitions Librarian with Gelman Library, at the George Washington University, in Washington, DC 20052.

appraisals. The 1986 tax legislation reversed the previous regulations by returning to requirements that only donors who itemize their deductions are entitled to tax deductions for non-cash charitable contributions.[1]

LIBRARIES AND GIFTS

Many public and private libraries have suffered from budget cutbacks and inflationary materials costs over the past few years, which has resulted in an increased dependence on gifts of materials for collections building. Libraries and their parent institutions have been in a state of flux in their attempts to keep up with the changing gift tax legislation. They have been constantly adjusting administrative policies and records systems, as well as attempting to provide essential information about IRS regulations to prospective donors.

By 1987, many institutions were concerned that the reduced tax incentives and increased reporting requirements would discourage donors of non-cash gifts. There is no indication that this happened; in fact, it is possible that charitable contributions have continued since so many other types of tax deductions have been disallowed. It is, however, assumed that acknowledgement requests for tax purposes of smaller gift donations (especially at year-end) have significantly declined.

An excellent survey was conducted in 1987 by the American Library Association Rare Books & Manuscripts Section, Ad Hoc Legislative Information Committee to assess the impact of the new regulations on American libraries. The survey supports the contention that there has not been a significant effect on library gift solicitations.[2]

The exception to this continues to be limited donations of works from living authors. In 1969, tax legislation specifically prohibited authors' tax deduction for the fair market value of a donation of their personal works. The deduction is still limited only to the cost of the materials used to produce the work since the provision was intended to deny public officials a tax advantage for works created with public funds. Nineteen eighty-seven and 1988 attempts to reverse the legislation with the "National Heritage Resource Act" have not been successful. Library surveys have shown that this regulation has continued to have a significant impact on donations of personal manuscripts by living authors.[3]

IRS REGULATIONS FOR NON-CASH CHARITABLE CONTRIBUTIONS

The following offers a brief outline of the Internal Revenue Service's reporting requirements to serve as a guide to forms and information.[4] The revised tax laws have reduced the number of donors likely to qualify for itemized deductions due to increases in the standard deduction and decreases in the actual tax rates. For example, the single standard deduction has increased from $2,480 in 1986 to $3,000 in 1988. The tax rates have diminished from 0-50% in 1986 to 11%-33% in 1988. These factors have combined to lessen the likelihood that donors will qualify for itemized deductions and the value of a deduction has diminished with the decline in the tax rates.[5]

1. Internal Revenue Service Form 8283 — Noncash Charitable Contributions

Donors must file Form 8283 (see Figure 1) if claiming a deduction for all non-cash gifts totaling more than $500 within a calendar year.

A. Donations of $500 or Less (within an aggregate gift of more than $500)

Side one, Section A (Part I) is to be completed for any items or groups of similar items for which the donor claims a deduction of $500 or less. There is an option to provide donee information, description of property, acquisition date, and method of acquisition, donor's cost, and fair market value determination for items valued at $500 or less. If the donor contributed a similar gift to another donee or if the donor designated restrictions on the donee's use of the property, further information is required in Part II.

FIGURE 1

Noncash Charitable Contributions

Form **8283**
(Rev. August 1988)

Department of the Treasury
Internal Revenue Service

▶ Attach to your Federal income tax return if the total claimed deduction for all property contributed exceeds $500.
▶ **See separate Instructions.**

OMB No. 1545-0908
Expires 3-31-90

Attachment
Sequence No. **55**

Name(s) as shown on your income tax return

Identification number

Note: *Compute the amount of your contribution deduction before completing Form 8283. (See your tax return instructions.)*

Section A	Include in Section A **only** items (or groups of similar items) for which you claimed a deduction of $5,000 or less per item or group, and certain publicly traded securities (see Instructions).

Part I Information on Donated Property

1	(a) Name and address of the donee organization	(b) Description of donated property (attach a separate sheet if more space is needed)
A		
B		
C		
D		
E		

Note: *Columns (d), (e), and (f) do not have to be completed if the amount you claimed as a deduction for the item is $500 or less.*

	(c) Date of the contribution	(d) Date acquired by donor (mo., yr.)	(e) How acquired by donor	(f) Donor's cost or adjusted basis	(g) Fair market value	(h) Method used to determine the fair market value
A						
B						
C						
D						
E						

40

Part II Other Information—Complete question 2 if you gave less than an entire interest in property listed in Part I.
Complete question 3 if restrictions were attached to a contribution listed in Part I.

2 If less than the entire interest in the property is contributed during the year, complete the following:

(a) Enter letter from Part I which identifies the property _____. (Attach a separate statement if Part II applies to more than one property.)

(b) Total amount claimed as a deduction for the property listed in Part I for this tax year _____ ;
for any prior tax year(s) _____ .

(c) Name and address of each organization to which any such contribution was made in a prior year (complete only if different from the donee organization above).

Charitable organization (donee) name
_____

Number and street
_____

City or town, state, and ZIP code
_____

(d) The place where any tangible property is located or kept. _____

(e) Name of any person, other than the donee organization, having actual possession of the property. _____

3 If conditions were attached to any contribution listed in Part I, answer the following questions:

	Yes	No
(a) Is there a restriction either temporarily or permanently on the donee's right to use or dispose of the donated property? .		
(b) Did you give to anyone (other than the donee organization or another organization participating with the donee organization in cooperative fundraising) the right to the income from the donated property or to the possession of the property, including the right to vote donated securities, to acquire the property by purchase or otherwise, or to designate the person having such income, possession, or right to acquire?		
(c) Is there a restriction limiting the donated property for a particular use?		

For Paperwork Reduction Act Notice, see separate Instructions.

Form **8283** (Rev. 8-88)

41

FIGURE 1 (continued)

Form 8283 (Rev. 8-88)

Name(s) as shown on your income tax return | Identification number

Section B **Appraisal Summary**—Include in Section B only items (or groups of similar items) for which you claimed a deduction of more than $5,000 per item or group. *(Report contributions of certain publicly traded securities only in Section A.)*

If you donated art, you may have to attach the complete appraisal. See the **Note** in Part II below.

Part I **Donee Acknowledgment** *(To be completed by the charitable organization.)*

1 This charitable organization acknowledges that it is a qualified organization under section 170(c) and that it received the donated property as described in Part II on _____

(Date)

Furthermore, this organization affirms that in the event it sells, exchanges, or otherwise disposes of the property (or any portion thereof) within two years after the date of receipt, it will file an information return (**Form 8282,** Donee Information Return) with the IRS and furnish the donor a copy of that return. This acknowledgment does not represent concurrence in the claimed fair market value.

Charitable organization (donee) name | Employer identification number

Number and street | City or town, state, and ZIP code

Authorized signature | Title | Date

Part II **Information on Donated Property** *(To be completed by the taxpayer and/or appraiser.)*

2 Check type of property:

☐ Art* (contribution of $20,000 or more)   ☐ Real Estate   ☐ Gems/Jewelry   ☐ Stamp Collections

☐ Art* (contribution of less than $20,000)   ☐ Coin Collections   ☐ Books   ☐ Other

*Art includes paintings, sculptures, watercolors, prints, drawings, ceramics, antique furniture, decorative arts, textiles, carpets, silver, rare manuscripts, historical memorabilia, and other similar objects. **Note:** *If you donated art after December 31, 1987, and your total art contribution deduction was $20,000 or more, you must attach a complete copy of the signed appraisal and include an 8 x 10 inch color photograph (or a color transparency, no smaller than 4 x 5 inches).*

3	(a) Description of donated property (attach a separate sheet if more space is needed)	(b) If tangible property was donated, give a brief summary of the overall physical condition at the time of the gift	(c) Appraised fair market value
A			
B			
C			
D			

See Instructions

	(d) Date acquired by donor (mo., yr.)	(e) How acquired by donor	(f) Donor's cost or adjusted basis	(g) For bargain sales after 6/6/88, enter amount received	(h) Amount claimed as a deduction	(i) Average trading price of securities
A						
B						
C						
D						

Part III Taxpayer (Donor) Statement

—List any item(s) included in Section B, Part II, that is (are) separately identified in the appraisal as having a value of not more than $500 or less. See instructions.

I declare that the following item(s) included in Part II above has (have) to the best of my knowledge and belief an appraised value of not more than $500 (per item). *(Enter identifying letter from Part II and describe the specific item):* _____

Signature of taxpayer (donor) ▶   Date ▶

Part IV Certification of Appraiser *(To be completed by the appraiser of the above donated property.)*

I declare that I am not the donor, the donee, a party to the transaction in which the donor acquired the property, employed by, married to, or related to any of the foregoing persons, or an appraiser regularly used by any of the foregoing persons and who does not perform a majority of appraisals during the taxable year for other persons.

Also, I declare that I hold myself out to the public as an appraiser or perform appraisals on a regular basis; and that because of my qualifications as described in the appraisal, I am qualified to make appraisals of the type of property being valued. I certify the appraisal fees were not based upon a percentage of the appraised property value. Furthermore, I understand that a false or fraudulent overstatement of the property value as described in the qualified appraisal or this appraisal summary may subject me to the civil penalty under section 6701(a) (aiding and abetting the understatement of tax liability). I affirm that I have not been barred from presenting evidence or testimony by the Director of Practice.

Please Sign Here

Signature ▶	Title ▶	Date of appraisal ▶

Business address		Identification number

City or town, state, and ZIP code

43

B. Donations of More Than $5,000

If the donor is claiming a deduction for items or groups of similar items for more than $5,000, the donor is required to complete side two, Section B (Part II) with a similar description of the property. Also, if the donor gave a series of smaller gifts of similar property (e.g., books), whose aggregate value exceeds $5,000, to several donees, a separate Form 8283 is required for each contribution.

C. Donee Acknowledgement

Non-cash gifts of more than $5,000, or lesser valued elements of an aggregate gift of more than $5,000, also require acknowledgement by the donee in Section B, Part I. This acknowledgement must be signed by an official authorized to sign the organization's tax returns or a person specifically designated to sign Form 8283 within the organization. The donee should retain a copy of Section B for its records.

D. Donor Statement for Separate Donations of $500

The donor must complete Section B, Part III for any items valued at $500 or less. This statement relieves the donor from filing Form 8282 for any items the donee may dispose (see 2 below).

E. Appraisal

The donor is also required by Section B, Part II to obtain a qualified appraisal of the property value. The appraisal must be made no earlier than 60 days prior to the contribution. A separate Form 8283 and appraisal is required for each item except for a group of similar items (e.g., a group of books, or manuscripts, by the same author). The appraiser may also provide a group description for items totaling $100 or less. The appraiser must sign Part IV to be considered qualified.[6] Persons who cannot be qualified appraisers are listed in the Certification of Appraiser (Part IV). Basically, according to Form 8283, this includes anyone who is a party to the transaction: "I declare that I am not the donor, the donee, a party to the transaction in which the donor acquired the property, employed by, married to, or related to any of the foregoing persons, or an appraiser regularly used by any of the foregoing persons and who does not perform a majority of appraisals during the taxable year for other persons." In addition, the appraisal fee cannot usually be a percentage of the appraised value unless the fees were paid to certain nonprofit associations. A copy of the appraisal is generally not attached to Form 8283, but the donor and donee are advised to retain a copy of the appraisal for their records. An exception to this is for a deduction for art valued at $20,000 or more. In this instance, a complete copy of the appraisal and an 8 × 10 inch color photograph (or color transparency no smaller than 4 × 5 inches) must be attached to Form 8283.

The following information is suggested for inclusion in a qualified appraisal:

1. A description of the property in sufficient detail for a person who is not generally familiar with the type of property to ascertain that the property that was appraised is the property that was contributed.
2. The physical condition of tangible personal property.
3. Date of contribution.
4. Terms of any agreement or understanding between the donor and donee which relates to the use of the property or to the sale or other disposition of the property.
5. Name, address, and taxpayer identification number of the Qualified Appraiser and the person who employs the appraiser, if any.
6. Statement of the qualifications of the Qualified Appraiser.
7. A statement that the appraisal was prepared for income tax purposes.
8. The date on which the property was valued.
9. The appraised fair market value of the property on the date of contribution.
10. The method of valuation, such as income approach, market data approach, or the replacement cost-less depreciation approach.

11. The specific basis for the valuation, if any, such as specific comparable sales transactions.
12. A description of the fee arrangement between donor and appraiser.

2. Internal Revenue Service Form 8282 — Donee Information Return (Sale, Exchange, or Other Disposition of Donated Property)

Donees must complete Form 8282 (see Figure 2) if any part of a donation claimed at more than $5,000 (or a smaller element of more than $500 if included in an aggregate of more than $5,000) is sold, exchanged, or otherwise disposed of within two years. There are two general exceptions to filing Form 8282. If appraised items valued at $500 or less are listed separately on Form 8283-Section B (Part II), the donee is not required to complete Form 8282 if these items are disposed of within two years. The other exception is if the items are consumed or distributed for charitable purposes.

If the donee fails to report Form 8282 for disposal of appraised items valued at more than $500, the penalty is $50 for failure to file Form 8282 (it is not clear if this is for each item valued at more than $5,000). If the donee gave the property to another charitable organization, this successor donee must be identified on Form 8282. Failure to provide correct information about successor donees and property values is a $5 penalty for each failure.

3. Alternative Minimum Tax

The process of providing donor information is further complicated for high-income donors who are subject to the Alternative Minimum Tax (AMT). This affects the donations of highly valued items contributed by high-income donors. In these cases, the appreciated value of a deduction must be declared as income in computing the amount subject to AMT. When the donor's AMT income exceeds the exemptions, the taxable income is adjusted and includes many of the deductions frequently claimed by wealthy donors. For example, a $25,000 appraised book may require that the appreciated value be added back to the donor's Alternative Minimum Tax income. It is, of course, the donor's responsibility to be aware of the circumstances of his/her own tax liability.

LIBRARY CONCERNS

Libraries have experienced a variety of problems as a result of these regulations. The RBMS survey found that the most cited problem was that of keeping up to date with changes to the regulations.[7] It is the frontline gifts staff who must undertake the daily consequences of gift transactions through providing donor and appraisal information and arranging for storage and disposal. It is important to summarize clearly the IRS requirements to donors who wish to claim a deduction for their contribution. The Certification of Appraiser in Form 8283 makes it explicit that the library may not perform an appraisal, or hire and have any regular association with the appraiser. In the past, it has been quite common for a library to pay for an appraisal of a generous gift, as well as frequently to refer donors to an antiquarian bookseller whom the library regularly uses for appraisal services. It is necessary for the library to be aware that the appraisal process will take place. When the final appraisal is received, it should be examined for possible problems such as general descriptions for groups of diverse items which may warrant separate appraisals. The donor is responsible for the appraisal and for providing support for the claimed fair market value; however, as the recipient, the library may wish to ease this process for the donor. Providing the donor with a referral to local appraisers and an outline of what action is required is usually appreciated.

The space limitations in many libraries have restricted the amount of material gifts they are able to accept. The backlog of gift storage and processing can become unmanageable without careful preliminary review and selection of gifts. The storage problem is compounded by the regulations for reporting disposal of gifts for which the library completed a Form 8283, Section B, Part I. It is an extremely delicate proposal to discuss disposal of a gift with prospective donors. It is advantageous for the library to avoid having to file Form 8282 in order not to offend donors, but at the same time the library will want to avoid housing thousands of unwanted volumes.

FIGURE 2

Form **8282**

(Rev. August 1988)

Department of the Treasury
Internal Revenue Service

Donee Information Return

(Sale, Exchange, or Other Disposition of Donated Property)

▶ See Instructions on back.

OMB No. 1545-0908
Expires 3-31-90

Give Copy to Donor

	Charitable organization (donee) name	Employer identification number
Please		
Print	Number and street	
or		
Type	City or town, state, and ZIP code	

Note: *If you are the original donee, DO NOT complete Part II, or column (c) of Part III*

Part I Information on ORIGINAL DONOR, and DONEE YOU GAVE THE PROPERTY TO

1(a) Name of the original donor of (first person to give) the property

Complete 2(a)–2(d) only if you gave this property to another charitable organization (successor donee):

2(a) Name of charitable organization	(b) Identification number (EIN)
(c) Address (number and street)	
(d) City or town, state, and ZIP code	

Part II Information on PREVIOUS DONEES—Complete this part only if you were not the first donee to receive the property. If you were the second donee, leave item 4 blank. If you were a third or later donee, then complete both items 3 and 4. In item 4 give information on the preceding donee (the one who gave you the gift).

3(a) Name of original donee	(b) Identification number (EIN)
(c) Address (number and street)	
(d) City or town, state, and ZIP code	

48

4(a) Name of preceding donee

(b) Identification number (EIN)

....

(c) Address (number and street)

(d) City or town, state, and ZIP code

Part III Information on DONATED PROPERTY

(a) Description of donated property sold, exchanged, or otherwise disposed of (attach a separate sheet if more space is needed)	(b) Date you received the item(s)	(c) Date the first donee received the item(s) (if you weren't the first)	(d) Date item(s) sold, exchanged, or otherwise disposed of	(e) Amount received upon disposition

For Paperwork Reduction Act Notice, see instructions on back.

Form **8282** (Rev. 8-88)

The library may wish to establish guidelines for accepting temporary or "loaned" gifts. If the gift has potential to become permanently donated, the library may want to arrange for a donation contract for a limited period. All agreements between the library and a prospective donor should be written and readily accessible.

Another problem area which requires flexibility is consideration of the Alternative Minimum Tax. AMT will have an effect on extremely valuable gifts contributed by wealthy donors. This was recently demonstrated by John Whitney Payson's sale of his Van Gogh "Irises" instead of donating it to the college where it had hung due to the potential cost of a donation. It is possible to spread donations over several years for upper income donors in order to assist them with possible AMT income adjustments. This requires very careful record-keeping on an annual basis with the donor and it is best to utilize a deposit donation contract or deed of gift.

Solicited gifts are easier to manage in that the library has the opportunity to discuss and review the collection with the donor, as well as plan storage, timing, and records. It is not uncommon for well-meaning administrators and faculty to accept valuable gift collections and leave the burden of appraisals and tax records to lower-level staff.

ADMINISTRATIVE POLICY

It is most important for the entire organization to have a clearly defined policy for non-cash contributions. Gifts staff should be familiar with their institution's policy and follow administrative guidelines for authorization to sign the Form 8283. It is recommended that policies include designated personnel for gifts acceptance and acknowledgement, as well as appraisal information. A deed of gift serves as a document describing the gift conveyance, donor ownership statement and signature, receipt date of gift and donee signature; in essence, it provides a record of the property transfer as well as documenting any use restrictions. Within a very large organization, records management may be the responsibility of more than one department. Many institutions require a gifts "log" in order to provide a record of all incoming gifts, whether solicited or unsolicited; accepted or rejected.

DONOR RELATIONS

When a library is contacted by a potential donor, it is most important to offer guidelines and information, while maintaining objectivity. It is necessary that the library avoid making the donor's own decision about qualification for tax deductions. The library can provide information to the donor, but it is always preferable to refer them to their own tax and legal advisors. The Rare Books and Manuscripts Section has now formed a new group to develop standard informational guidance through the RBMS Ad Hoc Gifts and Appraisals Brochure Committee.[8] This brochure will be helpful to libraries who do not already have informational handouts for prospective donors.

Suggested information to establish during the "interview" of a donor may include:

— Ask who they are; inquire about their affiliation and status with the institution.
— Assess the size, scope, and content of the collection.
— Discuss the library's selection policies and collection development procedures.
— Discuss donor's need for acknowledgement and any intention to claim a deduction for the gift donation. (If it is a substantial gift, the library will need to follow up with appraisal referral, deed of gift, and Form 8283.)
— Discuss the library's rights to disposal.
— Maintain gift files and records.

When it is known that the library may not collect materials in certain subjects, it is helpful to refer the donor to other libraries and organizations in the area who may wish to consider the gift.

CONCLUSION

The management of large gift operations can be an exciting collections building venture. It establishes continuing good public relations, as well as potential cash donations for the institution overall.

Unwanted gift materials can be utilized for gift book sales or sent to other organizations.

The library has a legal obligation to follow IRS regulations and provide correct information. Further, the library has an ethical obligation to avoid conflict of interest with prospective donors, especially in following the regulations for appraisals. With a clearly defined gifts policy statement, informational instruction, and good donor relations, libraries can develop successful and rewarding gift acquisition operations.

NOTES AND REFERENCES

1. *The Deficit Reduction Act of 1984*. Division A: Tax Reform Act of 1984. U.S. House of Representatives Report No. 98-861. 98th Congress (1984). Tax Reform Act of 1986, PL 99-514, enacted October 1986. Final regulations appear in *Federal Register* 53, No. 87 (May 5, 1988).

2. "The Tax Reform Act of 1984 and American Research Libraries," *C&RL News* (October 1988), pp. 589-91. Timothy Murray, compiler.

3. Excerpt from "Special Collections Resources: Implications of Current Legislation on Research," unpublished paper by William Keller presented at American Library Association, ACRL Legislation Committee Program, New Orleans, LA, July 1988.

4. For further information refer to "Instructions for Form 8283" (Revised August 1988); and Internal Revenue Service Publications: Number 526 "Charitable Contributions (for individuals)," Number 561 "Determining the Value of Donated Property," Number 544 "Sales and Other Dispositions of Assets" (for contributions of depreciable property), and Number 553 "Highlights of the Tax Changes" (revised December 1986, 1987 and 1988).

5. Klott, Gary L. *The New York Times Complete Guide to the New Tax Law*. New York: Times Books, 1986.

6. For further explanation of appraisal definitions, see Internal Revenue Service Regulations 1.170A-13(c)(3)(i)-(ii).

7. *C&RL News, Op. cit.*

8. For more information contact the American Library Association, Rare Book & Manuscript Section, Ad Hoc Gifts and Appraisals Brochure Committee.

Gifts —
The Answer to a Problem

Thomas C. White, III
J. Michael Morgan
Gus A. Gordon

SUMMARY. The informational demands made upon our libraries are growing at ever increasing rates. Yet, the monetary flow to pay for these demands is not keeping up with our library's needs. A viable fiscal solution could be to turn to our library's users for gifts. This article discusses the current income and estate tax opportunities that can be used to solicit contributions to our libraries. In addition this article defines the responsibilities of the acquisition librarian in this solicitation process.

INTRODUCTION

The purpose of the information presented below is to acquaint acquisition librarians with the tax effects of gifts and donations. Gifts and donations offer an opportunity for growth beyond the institutional budget. In recent years, institutional budgets have presented both difficult planning issues and some perplexing problems to those responsible for acquiring and maintaining a modern library. Some current, and often frustrating, questions that must be answered by the librarian today are:

Thomas C. White, III is Associate Professor in Accounting and Taxation; J. Michael Morgan is Associate Professor in Economics; Gus A. Gordon is Assistant Professor in Accounting and Auditing; all of the School of Business Administration and Economics at College of Charleston in Charleston, SC.

a. How does the acquisition librarian resolve the problem of either a decreasing budget or a budget that does not permit the library to remain current with today's quantity, quality, and technological needs?
b. What is the acquisition librarian's legal and practical responsibility for the solicitation of gifts and contributions?
c. How should the acquisition librarian approach the opportunity of charitable gifts to the library?

Many libraries currently face the problem of allocating very scarce (and often declining) resources in such a manner that the technical and informational needs of users are satisfied as best as possible. Since the 1960s, information and the need for information has been growing. Increasing a library's financial resources as well as gifts-in-kind would certainly help to resolve the problem of limited funding.

As librarians strive for economies and savings through the use of consortium and joint-power agreements, fiche and computer technology could, in the long-run, reduce acquisition and operational costs. But the acquisition of fiche and sophisticated computer technology requires funds. Gifts, by their non-repetitive nature, may be one way to secure an injection of funds necessary for the implementation of programs and processes that make the library more cost-efficient.

The library's consuming public seems to be rapidly expanding in its ever-increasing demand for information. There is the opinion that computer technology is both the cause of and the answer to these increasing demands. But computer technology is not inexpensive, and so, in order to service the public, substantial costs may have to be incurred. Gifts to the library may provide the funding for the acquisition of both computer hardware and software.

BASIC TAX CONSIDERATIONS

Those from whom libraries may solicit and potentially receive gifts are primarily of three types: (1) individuals, (2) corporations, and (3) associations. An association may include other charities, subdivisions of government, and the boards and library-friendly groups not functioning within the definitional confines of individuals or corporations.

Each of the three categories of contributors has legal restrictions placed upon it by the *Internal Revenue Code*, as now amended. Some of these restrictions address such questions as: (1) Who might receive charitable gifts? (2) How much of the charitable gift can the contributor deduct from current year income taxes? (3) If the gift in the current year exceeds the statutory limit on charitable contributions, can any excess be carried forward to future years and thereby reduce future taxable income? The answers to these questions are rather technical, and any problems must be resolved between the contributor and the contributor's tax advisor.

Since acquisition librarians frequently become involved with the decision-making process, the librarian should be aware of some very broad rules currently established by the Internal Revenue Service. An individual can give to charities and deduct, usually, up to fifty percent of their adjusted gross income during a particular year. If the value of the contribution exceeds fifty percent of their adjusted gross income for the year that the gift is made, then there are carry-over rules that may apply. The gift in excess of the fifty percent rule may be deducted during the five successive years after the year of the gift. Corporations, on the other hand, have a limit on charitable deductions of 10 percent of their taxable income. This 10 percent limit is for taxable income before any deduction for the charitable gift, as well as other special deductions, are made.[1,2] Corporations also have the five year carry-forward process that permits the donor to deduct a greater portion of the charitable gift. Gifts from associations are usually contributions without limit. The *Internal Revenue Code* encourages other charitable donors to give as much as possible and as soon as possible. There can, in fact, be penalties and fines imposed on those associations that attempt to accumulate large amounts of funds before making their contribution. These fines and penalties hasten the disposition of gifts to the charity receiver.

The expressed purpose of Congress with its enactment of the charitable contributions statutes was to assist governments, educational institutions, those social institutions that promoted the general public welfare, and the like. This assistance often permitted the extension of certain government programs that otherwise would be limited in nature and scope of operation.[3] Those charitable contributions that promote an extension of already existing government programs, in effect, relieve some of the burdens and responsibilities of government, and so the *Internal Revenue Code* not only allows charitable contributions as a deduction against gross income (taxable income falls) but the *Code* actually encourages charitable gifts in many cases. Public libraries are an example where contributions reduce the real expense to local governments of acquiring and maintaining an extensive and current set of information.

As an example of how an individual or corporation might enjoy considerable tax savings through charitable gifts consider the following example. A single taxpayer with a taxable income in the range between $43,150 and $89,560 has a marginal tax rate of 33 percent. This means that for each extra dollar of income earned by the individual, 33 cents is paid in Federal income taxes. Although state income tax brackets vary, assume that the individual considered here is in the ten percent bracket; each extra dollar of earned income nets ten cents for the state. So, this individual pays 43 cents in taxes for each extra dollar of income that is earned. If the individual contributed $100,000 to a library for a study room, then taxable income would be reduced by $43,000 and tax liability would fall by $43,000. This is a substantial tax saving. The Federal and State governments actually subsidize the study room by accepting a reduced taxable income and hence a reduced tax revenue. Also, an individual donor's estate could save up to 55 percent in Federal estate taxes with a comparable saving in the related state estate and/or inheritance taxes if a gift is bequeathed to a library.

A corporation with a taxable income between $100,000 and $335,000 has a marginal tax rate of 39 percent. If it is assumed that the corporate taxpayer has the same ten percent state tax rate as did the individual described above, then 49 cents out of each additional taxable dollar earned by the corporation is paid to government as taxes. A gift of $100,000 by the corporation for a study room would reduce its tax liability by $49,000.

Those institutions that are eligible to receive charitable gifts are well-defined by the *Code*.[4] Libraries as charitable recipients can be divided into two major categories. First, there are the public libraries that function as a subdivision of some level of government, and so they have automatic charitable status. Public libraries include those supported by city or county governments as well as those associated with public schools and colleges. The charitable recipient status for public libraries is rather automatic, and this status is accepted by taxing authorities. The second category is private libraries. Private libraries may become charitable recipients in their own right or they may qualify as a charitable recipient because they are part of a larger charitable organization. An example of this second type of recipient is the library on the campus of a private college. In the second category, the library will probably be listed in an annual cumulative listing of charitable organizations, and so the librarian may easily determine the tax-exempt status of the library by referencing its inclusion in the annual listing.[5]

In either of the above categories, the librarian should determine the organization's status by questioning the chief financial officer to see if the organization is included under Section 501(c) of the *Internal Revenue Code*.

TYPES OF GIFTS AND THEIR SIGNIFICANCE

Gifts can be categorized into several different types, but for ease of understanding two broad general categories are presented here:

1. Money and other highly liquid assets that can be given either in the current period or deferred until some later period, and
2. Properties that can be given either in the current period or deferred until some later period.

Money (cash or negotiable assets) can be given now or may be given in the future (deferred). If money is given now, it is an especially welcome gift because of its current market (spendable) value. Since money is the most liquid of assets, it is easily used. Money payment in the future or a flow of money payments in the future is a deferred gift. This deferral often occurs when the library has been named the income beneficiary of an estate or trust. When a gift of money or other liquid assets is deferred until some future time period, its current value and its future value are not necessarily the same. The current value of the asset may very well be less than its future value. Deferred assets must be evaluated at their current value even though they will not be received until some later period. The stream of payments in the future, or a single future payment, may come from outright gifts, assigned annuities, grants, royalties, life insurance policies, pooled income funds, and unitrusts. Currently there are literally millions of small life insurance policies that are forgotten but are still in force. An example is the life insurance policies issued by the Veterans Administration after World War II and the Korean War. These policies, if given now, could result in an immediate tax savings to the donor.

Properties, which are less liquid can also be given now or deferred as a bequest. These properties include items such as books, journals, manuscripts, as well as rare artifacts. Properties also include land, buildings, equipment that is used by the library, and the like. These properties, since they are not the most liquid of assets, have an accompanying evaluation problem. In addition, there are the business or corporate donors who may contribute inventories or technical items such as computers, computer software, and any required installation. Furthermore, there may be an additional problem of whether there really is a gift, or whether a donation is simply the donor dumping unwanted materials. If a donation is not made in good faith, special problems arise when a value must be placed on the gift.

RECEIPT AND RECOGNITION OF THE GIFT

Acquisition librarians are the individuals best qualified to render an opinion on the value of any properties received by the library. Money and other highly liquid assets generally pose no evaluation problem since their value is simply the face value of the asset.

Other properties, however, may very well require an appraisal. When an asset is donated to a library and its value must be determined, the appraisal must reflect the asset's fair market value; it cannot be a sham appraisal. The *Internal Revenue Code* has specified some severe penalties for sham appraisals.[6] If the donor wants to reduce taxable income by more than the fair market value of the gift, and if the appraiser assists by inflating the appraisal, then the appraiser has assisted in the perpetration of a sham and has violated the law as well as the intent of Congress.

Any estimate of the value of a gift should be the fair market value of the asset. Fair market value is defined as: "The amount at which the property would change hands between a willing buyer and a willing seller, neither being under any compulsion to buy or sell and both having reasonable knowledge of the relevant facts."[7] The real response to the question of what is fair market value of an item is the amount that you would be willing to pay for the item.

Ideally, the Internal Revenue Service should receive a detailed evaluation of each item that is appraised, or in the case of a collection, a detailed evaluation of the appraisal of the collection itself. Outside assistance should be sought in determining the gift's fair market value. When a special appraisal is required to determine the value of a gift, it is the taxpayer's (donor's) responsibility to obtain and pay for this appraisal. In the event that a special appraisal is required and the donor must pay for this appraisal, the costs incurred by the donor are deductible as a Miscellaneous Expense on Schedule A of the 1040 Form.

There is an exception for corporations and other types of businesses in that if they contribute properties which to them are classified as inventories or depreciable business assets, the property's value for gift purposes is usually the same as the businesses' basis in the property.

Gifts to libraries can also be such items as computers, installed computing systems, computer software, buildings and improvements to existing buildings, and the like. The correct evaluation of such gifts is the dollar value that it would have cost the library to purchase the items in the market.

When a library or other charitable institution receives a gift of property, there is an extra set of rules especially enforced by the Internal Revenue Service regarding the retention and disposal of the property.[8] These rules fall into two broad categories. First, if the gift has a fair market value in excess of $5,000, then detailed records of the receipt of the gift must be maintained. The records should specifically state (a) the name and address of the donor, (b) the date that the gift was made and the institution received ownership or control of the gift, and (c) an appraisal and value of the gift must be maintained. The second rule applies to the disposition of a gift. If there is a subsequent disposition of any donated properties within two years of the date that the gift was made, it is necessary for the recipient to notify the Internal Revenue Service of the information maintained under the first rule above as well as the disposition value. Failure to notify the Internal Revenue Service may result in substantial penalties being imposed on the charitable institution. This notification will, of course, alert the Internal Revenue Service of any initial excessive evaluation of the donated gift.

Once a gift has been made and the recipient has clear and complete control of the gift, a letter of appreciation containing both the date of receipt and a statement of an appraised fair market value of the gift should be sent to the contributor. The appropriate individual to send the letter of appreciation could be either the acquisition librarian or the head of library services.

CONCLUSIONS

Whether public or private, most libraries in the nation have been designated by the Internal Revenue Service as a tax exempt organization and a charitable receiver. Currently the tax laws promote the donation of gifts to charitable institutions; one of the themes of the Reagan Administration was that institutions should rely on private rather than public support. To assist in any solicitation process that the library might undertake, individual taxpayers could very well experience a 43 percent tax saving for every dollar that they contribute. Corporations will quite often experience an even greater tax savings for every dollar that they contribute.

Most libraries have access to specialized talent that would be pleased to assist in fund-raising campaigns. Tax attorneys and certified public accounts, for instance, might visit the library quite frequently, and they are very interested in the library's reference resources. Perhaps the advisory board could consist of some financial and legal specialists who would be willing to offer their assistance and expertise. Public libraries can often secure the services of their in-house counsel, and they usually have access to the services of city or county financial experts. The resources are there for the library to undertake effective fund-raising campaigns. What has to be done is to inform the public in general, and potential donors in particular, about the tax advantages of contributing either funds or real properties to the library. Our society is driven by the creation and dissemination of information, and libraries are the guardians of our knowledge.

REFERENCES

1. *Internal Revenue Code of 1986*, as amended, Section 170, "Charitable, Etc. Contributions and Gifts."
2. *Internal Revenue Regulations*, Section 1.170A-11.
3. *Internal Revenue Code of 1986*, as amended, Section 4942.
4. *Ibid.*, Section 501(C).
5. *Cumulative List, Organizations Described in Section 170 (c) of the Internal Revenue Code*, Internal Revenue Service Publication No. 78, current edition.
6. *Internal Revenue Service Regulations*, Section 1.170A-13.
7. *Internal Revenue Service Regulations*, Section 20.2031-1(G).
8. *Internal Revenue Code of 1986*, as amended, Section 6050(L).

The Legalities of Acquiring Software for an Academic Library

Joyce L. Ogburn

SUMMARY. This article gives a definition of software and an introduction to some of the legal problems of acquiring different types of software. The role of policies for acquisition of this type of material is stressed.

INTRODUCTION

Academic libraries across the country are faced with meeting the growing need for patron access to electronic resources. Libraries, committed to developing teaching and research collections, may endeavor to treat software as much like other library material as possible. In reality, since libraries represent a fairly small share of the market, software development and distribution does not occur with library needs in mind. Therefore, libraries must realize that the nature of software and the software industry necessitates special handling.

As libraries turn toward building software collections, acquisitions librarians must be ready to deal with the complex legal issues which surround the process of acquiring of software. Acquisitions librarians must achieve a high level of expertise in dealing with the ethics and legalities of software, for we often are the librarians who will encounter the registration cards, warranties, copyright statements, and license agreements. Are we prepared to handle the acquisition of this new medium?

Joyce L. Ogburn is Order Librarian with Pattee Library, Pennsylvania State University, University Park, PA 16802.

DEFINITION OF SOFTWARE

First, a good understanding of software is required. Most people think of software as the programs and data that come on floppy disks to be used on microcomputers. Actually, software can encompass much more. Software is definable as all the programs, procedures, and data used for the operation of a computer system. Programs and procedures, which operate the computer hardware and manipulate data include operating systems, assemblers, translators, compilers, generators, applications programs, subroutine libraries, and utility programs. Data can consist of relatively unstructured collections of data elements or highly organized, structured records. This definition of software includes material on floppy disks, microdisks, machine-readable data files, laser disks, and CD-ROM.

An institution may handle the acquisition of these forms of software through various purchasing units. The library may not be involved in acquiring machine-readable data files on tape, but instead may purchase only floppy disks and CD-ROM. Often these forms of software have some legal restrictions on their use or have license agreements. Librarians must acquaint themselves with all of the available software formats and their potential legal entanglements.

LEGAL ASPECTS OF ACQUIRING SOFTWARE

Having software in an academic library involves more complicated handling than most other materials, primarily because of legal issues. Several basic types of software, with varying levels of legal restrictions, exist:

1. Public domain software—This type of software has no legal restrictions and is uncopyrighted. The acquirer may modify, copy, and distribute the software.
2. Shareware software—Shareware is much like public domain software. Its producer's primary concern is to distribute the software to a wide audience relatively cheaply. The software developer may request a small fee for using the software or for acquiring full documentation. Shareware may be copyrighted.
3. Copyrighted software—No restrictions govern this software

other than copyright law, which prohibits copying and modifying without permission. Under copyright law, software is considered a literary work. Purchasers must honor the copyright law as they would for other copyrighted material. Most software is copyrighted, except for that in the public domain.
4. Software with license agreements—Licenses do not grant ownership of the software, but grant the licensee permission to use the software under the conditions of the agreement. The software remains the property of the licensor. License agreements generally prohibit the transfer of the software to any other party by gift, sale, or other means without permission of the licensor. Licenses may be in effect for a limited time and may need renewal. Often the license agreement restricts use of the software to a single site, variously defined as a computer, a building, a geographic location, or an institution. The agreement may not define site clearly. It may take effect with the opening of the package (usually by breaking a seal or removing the shrink wrap). The licensee may be required to sign and return the license agreement. Licensed software programs usually are copyrighted.

In addition, the software may come with warranty and/or registration cards. These do not govern the use of the software; instead their purpose is to register the software owner's name with the company for providing support, updates, or replacements.

The American Library Association, in conjunction with the National Education Association, has produced an excellent guide to copyright, which contains a substantial section on software.[1] It answers a great many questions about the application of copyright law to software.

EDUCOM, a consortium of institutions and businesses concerned with educational computing and technology, sponsored the production of a more comprehensive guide to the management of software in the academic setting.[2] It gives a detailed account of legal and management issues which are essential to policy formation. Only a small section mentions libraries, but the book as a whole provides useful information for any academic library planning to add software to its collections. EDUCOM continues to provide leadership in exploring academic computing issues.

THE ROLE OF POLICIES

Given the complexity of the legal issues, many academic institutions have developed wide-ranging policy statements on the ethical use of software and the consequences of inappropriate or unauthorized use of software. These statements can guide the library in policy development and implementation. Academic libraries must formulate clear and concise written policies on having software in the collections as protection against misuse by patrons and staff. In some cases, a library may have no general policy about how software is acquired, handled, cataloged, or circulated. When this is true, acquisitions should develop a policy which will allow the library to build a collection without encountering legal problems. Library policy should be written to encourage the collection, use, circulation, and preservation of software within the boundaries of the academic institution's policies, existing library policies, and legal restrictions.

Ideally, the collection development policies of every academic library should include a statement on collecting software. The requester of a software package should attempt to obtain a copy of the license agreement and review it for possible conflict with existing policies. If a library cannot comply with a valid, non-negotiable software license agreement, the software should not be purchased.

There are existing educational policies which may aid a library or acquisitions department in developing a software policy. One of them is the EDUCOM Code,[3] a statement on the ethical and legal use of software. Briefly summarized, it supports copyright law, the intellectual rights of software developers, and encourages the proper use of software. In 1986 the Association of Research Libraries published a SPEC Kit[4] which collected a group of microcomputer software policies in one document. Both the EDUCOM brochure and the SPEC kit provide invaluable information for guidance in constructing a policy.

ACQUISITIONS POLICIES

As previously noted, every acquisitions department purchasing software should have a written policy which addresses the acquisition of this material. Drafting an acquisitions policy is especially important for libraries without policies on software use. In this case, acquisitions may have to serve as the controlling unit to ensure that no software is acquired which cannot be used in compliance with the law and license agreements. Software, which can be acquired in much the same way as any other material, can greatly complicate the acquisition process. It is available through firm orders, approval plans, standing orders, subscriptions, blanket order, and memberships. The acquisitions department must understand the complexities of acquiring software and formulate policies and strategies which facilitate proper handling.

The most common way to acquire software is by firm order. To avoid legal problems peculiar to circulating software, it has been suggested that libraries order all software directly from the producer and state on the order form that the software is for library use and will be circulated.[5] This suggestion only works if acquisitions goes to the producer for all of its software purchases, bypassing discount houses or specialty vendors which may offer the software at a lower price. Going directly to the producer also restricts purchasing through the parent institution at favorable, volume discount prices. One advantage of going to the producer is that acquisitions might be able to find out the terms of any restrictions prior to the purchase of the software and negotiate better terms or prices.

Acquisitions also can obtain software through approval programs or form selection plans. The software may be part of a book or an independent item. Publishers sometimes provide software as part of a series or on subscription. Acquisitions may find that standing orders bring in the occasional software package. Memberships and blanket orders can also include software. Even software received in these ways may have restrictions on its use. Establish clear guidelines with library vendors as to whether software is desired.

Gifts of software from well-meaning donors should be accepted only if the library can comply with any restrictions stipulated by the software developer. When a license agreement states that ownership cannot be transferred without the permission of the producer, the potential donor cannot give it away, nor can the library accept it. Also, the library has almost no way of knowing whether illegal copies of that software exist and cannot protect itself against legal action. The library must not breach an agreement made by another party.

Some libraries may even wish to acquire software through exchange programs, computer user groups, or from electronic bulletin boards. Acquisitions should be prepared to deal with these strategies as well.

Acquisitions may want to investigate the possibility of negotiating with software producers for license agreements which suit the library environment. If collection development has determined the licensing restrictions on software before requesting its purchase, acquisitions will be on firmer ground in ordering the material. The easiest way to negotiate may be to work through the purchasing unit on campus already authorized to negotiate agreements. The parent institution also may maintain a list of software to which the institution has a site license or for which favorable negotiation has taken place. The terms of these agreements may be crucial to the library if it is considered part of the institutional site. The software may likely be purchased more cheaply or be circulated with few or no restrictions.

Regardless of how the material is acquired, someone must review all licensing arrangements for possible conflict with established institutional, library, and acquisitions policies. Someone must sign and keep copies of all agreements and contracts. The authority for review and record-keeping may be in acquisitions, the library's administrative office, the library computer services department, the computer center, or in the institution's purchasing department. The responsibility for these functions must be established.

Prior to acquiring the software, acquisitions usually has no knowledge of any license or legal restrictions attached. Acquisitions should train the receiving unit to handle carefully all software receipts. The staff must be able to identify any agreements and not open shrink-wrapped packages without the approval of the designated reviewer.

In addition to the concerns over the obvious legal issues, the library may need to limit purchases to software which can be run on library-controlled hardware, a condition which is necessary if a site license specifies the software be used in the library. Acquisitions also may have to purchase more than one copy to meet both demand and restrictions on software use.

There remains one more concern. If acquisitions purchases software for locations other than the library (e.g., the computer center or microcomputer labs), the authority of the library or the acquisitions department in contract negotiation or in prevention of the improper use of software must be spelled out in a policy statement.

When the acquisitions department is the official purchasing agent for the library, it may be accountable for the misuse of software. Obviously, acquisitions benefits from having a policy; however, since acquisitions is the department which first handles the software and reviews agreements, it may also serve as the watchdog for the library. An acquisitions policy can serve as protection for the library, as well as facilitating proper ordering and handling. Acquisitions may need to undertake the role of educator for the library to avoid software misuse by patrons and employees.

CONCLUSION

One cannot understate the importance of the academic library and its parent institution establishing clear policies on software use. If no such policies exist, acquisitions must develop a comprehensive policy for itself. If the library or institution does have policies, acquisitions still should have established guidelines and procedures for acquiring software. Staff, in addition to librarians, should be made aware of the challenges software presents. Legal restrictions are not to be taken lightly, and with careful planning and understanding of the issues, acquisitions can establish a successful program for acquiring software.

REFERENCES

1. Mary Hutchings Reed, *The Copyright Primer for Librarians and Educators* (Chicago: American Library Association; Washington: National Education Association, 1987).

    2. Shirley C. Smith, *Managing Academic Software: Leadership, Law and Logistics for Administrators, Faculty and Publishers* (McKinney, Texas: Academic Computing Publications, Inc., 1988).

    3. *Using Software: A Guide to the Ethical and Legal Use of Software for Members of the Academic Community* (Princeton: EDUCOM; Arlington, Va.: ADAPSO, 1987).

    4. *Microcomputer Software Policies in ARL Libraries*. ARL SPEC Kit #123. (Washington, D.C.: Association of Research Libraries, 1986).

    5. Reed, p. 48.

Taking License:
Librarians, Publishers
and the New Media

Meta Nissley

SUMMARY. Acquisitions librarians may find themselves signing lease or license agreements for library materials, particularly new media, which obligate the library to adhere to certain restrictive practices on the distribution and use of the material purchased. While librarians have been careful in supporting copyright law, some license agreements are more restrictive in nature than the provisions stated in the copyright law of 1976. Some libraries may have difficulty in adhering to those restrictions. The burden of enforcement of restrictions is placed on the library and librarians, not the vendor, publisher or user. Librarians must be aware of the content of lease/license agreements and what infringement entails when products are purchased and housed in libraries.

The nature of the acquisitions librarian's role is the "hunting and gathering" of information which can be distributed to the community the librarian serves. The business of acquiring and managing materials for library collections is becoming increasingly complex with the introduction of each new innovative format for disseminating information. While the majority of current purchases for most libraries still favors the traditional print format, acquisitions librarians have had to develop skills to handle newer formats. Over the years, nonprint media such as photographs, maps, videotapes and off-the-air taping presented unique challenges to acquire, store and distribute to the public at large. Software arrived on the scene with

Meta Nissley is Head of the Acquisitions and Collection Management with Meriam Library, California State University-Chico, Chico, CA 95929-0295.

an unparalleled explosion of public interest. Not only were libraries encouraged to provide software for public use, but to furnish the hardware and, in some cases, render assistance or instruction to users unfamiliar with the software programs or equipment. The demand for videotapes and software programs by the public placed libraries in the position of having to enforce copyright restrictions as both formats are conducive to copying when an original is easily accessible.

Although libraries have buckled down and obeyed copyright restrictions on the borrowing and photocopying of journal articles through interlibrary loan, this practice is far from resolving the issue of compensation to authors and publishers and providing broad access to information without overburdening library staff. The greatest burden as enforcers of restrictions on the use of information seems to be falling to libraries and librarians, not the publisher or the vendor. This trend is increasing as newer formats, and their accompanying restrictions, find their way to library shelves.

In traditional monographic and serial acquisitions rarely have librarians encountered the restrictions on purchase, use, and placement of materials which is now being seen with the newer technologies. The occasional restriction on copying information in printed sources appeared with the advent of photocopying machines in libraries. Some of these included asking librarians to hold drivers' licenses of users wanting to borrow, and potentially copy, certain works. Signs were posted in libraries, and other information centers informing the public of the copyright law and what infringement entailed. Since that time, other formats have been introduced into libraries requiring special consideration in the placement of the material, how it could be used, and what the library's responsibility is in providing users with information about restrictions on use and copying.

While the acquisitions librarian may not always have to contend with the issues at the public end, such as copying, he/she may be the person who signs off on the lease or license agreement for the product when it is purchased or leased. The acquisitions librarian must make every effort to provide materials to users without jeopardizing the intellectual property rights of others. As the complexity of purchasing or leasing resources for library users and collections increases, acquisitions librarians must familiarize themselves with the meaning of copyright protection and infringement and the language of contracts and agreements which accompany many of the newer products. While no suggestion is made here to require acquisitions librarians to attend law school and, please, leaving the drafting and legal interpretation of license agreements to the lawyers, it behooves a librarian to have at least a basic working knowledge of the issues and obligations involved in doing business in the information industry.

PROTECTING RIGHTS

Librarians consent to comply with copyright law by acknowledgement of certain practices, such as posting signs regarding infringement, and more formal acknowledgements in the form of signed agreements. License agreements tend to be more restrictive and protective of the publisher or producer than the protections provided by the copyright law.

Copyright Law

Speaking strictly from a non-legal point of view, general opinion of the current copyright law is that it is vague, ambiguous and confusing particularly as it applies to libraries, resource-sharing and fair use. The Copyright Act of 1976 has been left for the courts to interpret on a case-by-case basis. There have been some conflicting cases and decisions which have made distribution of information difficult for libraries. As an example, take the current use of videos in libraries, public and academic, and look at the confusion over what constitutes a "public performance." While a user may borrow a video from a library for home use, if the user chooses to view the video in the library it may be considered a "public performance" even though the user may be viewing it alone. As Ivan R. Bender states:

> Performance of a video in a public library requires a license. In my opinion, this is what the law says, and no distinction is made between viewing by an individual, a small group, or a larger group.[1]

Academic libraries may fall under the classroom exemption which allows showing of "home videos" in a not-for-profit classroom setting with an instructor present. However, if it is viewed in a carrel by a student without an instructor, the practice is still unclear and ambiguous as to whether this is truly infringement of copyright law. Hence, because of the uncertainty, some libraries pursue the granting of written permission by the producer to use home videos in a library setting.

What about "fair use"? The concept of "fair use" has been commonly interpreted by academic institutions and libraries to mean a reasonable number of copies, not in entirety, that may be copied for educational purposes without the express consent of the author of the work. The fair use of materials for educational purposes was addressed in the Copyright Law (Sections 107-118). "Fair use" has also become tangled in the web of the law and subject to interpretation and legal precedent. Obviously, most librarians maintain high ethical standards regarding copying of information without due compensation to the copyright holder. However, librarians are also educators and disseminators of information to a wide range of users including those in education and the scientific and technological fields where the transfer of information is key to conducting research. According to the Constitution, Congress shall have the power "to promote the progress of science and useful arts, by securing for limited times, to authors and inventors, the exclusive right to their respective writings and discoveries." Balance must be maintained between the flow of information and just compensation to copyright holders. Librarians appear to be a central part of the balancing act between the disseminating and the protecting of intellectual property.

Lease/License Agreements

One of the first questions a librarian asks upon receiving a lease or license agreement requiring an authorized signature is, "Why is a license required?"; which is usually then followed by, "What does my signature on the dotted line mean for me and the institution I am employed by?" Remember that license agreements are written by lawyers for publishers and producers of information packages.

They are not written for the protection of the rights of libraries or librarians. It is at the insistence of publishers, in a desire to have a document which may be valid in court in case of action in the event that protection as written in the copyright act is perceived or proven not to be strong enough for them, that librarians are obliged to sign license or lease agreements.

Almost any newer media which is acquired for the library collection today requires some acknowledgement or a license/lease agreement outlining restrictions on use and copying. Software programs, CD-ROMs, videodiscs and online services generally have agreements or contracts covering copyright protection and restrictions on use and distribution. Lease or license agreements define the terms and conditions acknowledged between parties, in this case, usually a library and a publisher, although provisions for a third party may be introduced in acknowledgement of public users at not-for-profit institutions. The license agreement a library sees may be the result of prior negotiations among the publisher, original copyright holder and wholesaler which influences the extent of restrictions a library must abide by.

Agreements may arrive in acquisitions departments in several ways, the most popular being a multi-copy form sent by the publisher or vendor upon receipt of a purchase order or subscription request which usually requires an authorized signature to be valid. "Shrink-wrap" licenses became popular with software programs where if the plastic packaging protecting a disk was broken or removed, the customer automatically agreed to comply with the restrictions listed. The customer did not always have the advantage of reading the conditions in advance. Another similar approach was taken by returning cards contained in software packages, requiring consent before assistance or updates would be given the customer, a subtle way, perhaps, of reminding us that libraries do not own the information contained on the disk. In some cases, for online data searching services, a written agreement is required and in others, information noting copyright protection and restrictions on use appears on the screen as one connects online. Believe it or not, there are still a few products which do not require agreements, but they are becoming rare. Several products which could be purchased years ago without agreements, currently require them. There are a few publishers who, as a marketing technique, are not bothering with license agreements.

Quite often a "boilerplate" or standard agreement is followed by publishers, making the task of reading and comprehending much less time consuming. Few boilerplate agreements address educational and not-for-profit institutions per se. Needs for specific institutions need to be negotiated within the framework of the agreement as it is presented to the library or the library may not be able to comply with the agreement or to purchase/subscribe to the product if negotiations are not successful.

The content of lease/license agreements varies with the format of the product and may vary from product to product within the same format. For instance, CD-ROM license agreements are becoming more standardized but still vary considerably from product to product regarding networking, downloading, archival copies of software, and general usage. When consenting to a license agreement with a publisher such as SilverPlatter or DIALOG, there may be unique terms and conditions for specific databases, CD-ROM or online, in addition to the general agreement. DIALOG has a "Database Supplier Conditions" list advising the consumer of the databases which may not be duplicated, stored, transferred electronically or mechanically, et cetera, and recommends obtaining permission from the database supplier for uses which may be protected under normal circumstances. It is doubtful that many librarians have been aware of or concerned about the restrictions regarding individual files on online databases. However, some, although not many, address specific responsibilities of educational institutions, libraries and librarians. For example, several very common databases produced by a scientific publisher state in their agreements, "Librarians and information brokers who are searchers may supply a single copy of search results, in print form or on magnetic media, to a client, but must insure that (the publisher's) copyright is known to these clients."

OBJECTIONS TO AGREEMENTS

A sampling of currently available lease/license agreements resulted in a surfacing of several key issues commonly found among them, which might be difficult for libraries to comply with. Some of the clauses in agreements which may cause particular concern for librarians are listed below. Not all agreements contain exactly the same language or specific content, but most of the elements are similar.

Ownership

A large proportion of licensing agreements are for a subscription to the use of the information, not its purchase. When data, discs, versions, et cetera, need to be updated, the superseded product must be returned according to most agreements. The issue of ownership is one that is getting more attention these days as libraries and information specialists look for solutions to long-term problems. How much of the resources available to users will be owned, and housed, in the library of the future? One of the factors complicating acquiring new media is the leasing of the information and the means to access it, rather than the outright purchase of the data itself. While the concept of neither owning nor housing information but rather being information brokers may be tangible in the future, acquisitions librarians are currently having to weigh carefully the lease versus purchase issue. For instance, if a subscription to a CD-ROM product in the medical field were begun, should the paper subscription be cancelled to offset the additional costs, and if so, how is retrospective data stored and retrieved if the CD-ROM subscription is cancelled at a later date and the discs returned as most publishers require? This could lead to a certain lack of confidence in a library's ability to develop its collection thoroughly.

Downloading

In an age when transference of information can be done electronically from machine to machine, users want to be able to take the information from a database, for instance, for temporary storage on a local terminal where it might be manipulated to suit the needs of the individual. For years, publishers and vendors have been unwilling to grant downloading rights to users. Current agreements will include restrictions to downloading such as "customer agrees to take all necessary action to restrict, control and limit the use of and access to products and to protect and secure products to prevent unauthorized copying, transfer or use." The question of "intent" on the part of the user arises with downloading. Is the purpose of downloading to pursue research or other quests of educational value or is it to repackage the data for commercial or other illegal uses? How would the librarian know, for instance, if the data were being misused, and furthermore, should the charge of a librarian include monitoring how information is used or misused? Recently, there have been some concessions by publishers of online, CD-ROM and software products allowing downloading, within limits, and almost exclusively within one institution. Hopefully, more publishers will loosen up on this restriction in the future.

Networking

Limitations to networking, both in-house and in local area networks (LANs) are usually found in agreements for software programs, databases and CD-ROMs. From a library perspective, it is logical, both in terms of access and cost-per-use, to disseminate data widely. Librarians with their service-oriented attitudes and public-minded spirits want to give information away to anyone who wants it. Naturally, this is incompatible with the needs of publishers who have invested considerable capital to create products, attempt to keep prices reasonable, but must sell or lease a certain number of each product to make it worth their while and serve as an incentive to produce more products in the future.

Applicable Law

Included in most lease/license agreements is a statement about which state's or country's laws govern the agreement. This tends to be the laws of the state where the publisher resides, but may be another state. If the governing law is from a state other than the one where the library is located, it could be a problem for the library to comply, particularly for institutions which must adhere to a specific state's laws.

Indemnification

This clause generally allows the publisher or producer of the product to be held harmless in the case of claims from the user.

Limits to Liability

Objectionable, at least in principle to librarians, is the clause which states that liability is disclaimed by the publisher for accuracy, completeness or functioning of the product and that the customer takes the product "as is." This is, supposedly, standard in agreements of this nature. However, it does little to inspire confidence in the quality and integrity of the product being leased or purchased.

In summary, objections may be raised regarding restrictive language in licensing agreements over the following: ownership, networking, downloading, copying, location, applicable law, indemnification and liability. Whether or not license agreements between publishers and librarians will stand up in court is not certain, but at this point in time librarians must take the terms and conditions of these agreements seriously until precedent is set otherwise.

Artistic License

When acquiring products such as software programs, using a waiver on a purchase order, such as "Vendor understands, acknowledges and agrees that (the educational institution) operates a lending library which regularly lends educational materials, including computer software, to faculty, students and other patrons" may be all that is needed to satisfy both the vendor and library. It also gives the vendor or publisher an opportunity at the beginning of the process to understand the ramifications of selling to a public institution. Occasionally, a vendor will find the waiver unacceptable and refuse to sell to the institution with an attached waiver or, perhaps, will ignore it and send a licensing agreement along with the product. How might an acquisitions librarian cope with a lease or license agreement, for any media, which is incompatible, at least in portions, with the guidelines provided by his/her institution?

One method which can be employed is the process of negotiation. The librarian can simply delete, rewrite, add to and otherwise change the document to suit the needs of the institution, and to provide protection for herself/himself. Publishers and vendors are motivated to lease or sell products rather than have a warehouse full of unused products. Consequently, changes made to licensing agreements are quite often readily accepted. Dialog with publishers is essential in working through difficult agreements.

Responsibility

What are the responsibilities of the librarian to inform the public and colleagues with respect to copyright protection and other restrictions found in licensing agreements? It is ethically sound to make an effort to distribute information regarding infringement on use of products found in the library environment. It could be a rather cumbersome process, however, to distribute warnings about each product's limitations. Posting signs in appropriate areas, having the user sign an acknowledgement form when borrowing media, educational programs and, above all, having a policy for the library regarding its obligations of informing the public are recommended precautions to stave off potential difficulties with copyright infringement and misuse of data.

Liability

Are librarians personally liable as employees of public institutions? Given the increasing number of lawsuits against public institutions, including libraries, many libraries carry liability and malpractice insurance. Protection of public institutions and their employees varies from state to state and is sometimes vague within specific regulations regarding interpretation pertaining to libraries. Under "sovereign immunity" institutions have been protected from suit by individuals; however, case law has established otherwise.[2] Precedent has also been set for persons employed by public institutions being held individually liable even if the institution is exempt from suit.

For acquisitions librarians there are at least three identifiable areas which could warrant caution and awareness in order to protect oneself from liability; outright responsibility for infringement of copyright law, non-compliance of a signed license agreement and knowingly passing on inaccurate information or data to users. Although possible, the likelihood of a librarian being sued for copyright infringement or violating a license agreement is probably minimal. After all, what would a publisher gain from litigation but bad publicity and little economic gratification? There is little precedent set as yet to check the validity of license/lease agreements in court.

CONCLUSION

If licensing agreements seem like a bad dream now, what does the future hold as more new technological innovations are introduced to the marketplace? Electrocopying and electronic transfer, in general, will present enormous problems to librarians and publishers. Collective agreements for licensing of software, databases and optical media are being investigated by United Kingdom and European publishers. Supporting and working with vendors and publishers to introduce new or unique solutions to contemporary acquisitions problems can only serve to smooth librarians' paths in the future. For the time being, however, lease/license agreements are an element in the process of purchasing newer media. It is incumbent upon the acquisitions librarian to investigate, negotiate and abide by licensing agreements for products accessed and housed within his or her library. Ultimately, it could be the librarian signing agreements for the library who is held responsible for the infringement by others. As stated in an acquisitions textbook,

> In his place in the microcosm of the library, the acquisitions librarian must face the fact that if all goes well, compliments will be few, and if anything goes amiss, complaints will be swiftly forthcoming.[3]

REFERENCES

1. Ivan R. Bender, "Copyright: Compromise or Confusion," *American Libraries* 20:2 (February 1989). p. 1113.
2. Joseph J. Mika and Bruce A. Shuman, "Legal Issues Affecting Libraries and Librarians. Lesson II: Liability insurance, malpractice and copyright," *American Libraries*, 19:2 (February 1988). pp. 108-112.

3. Theodore Grieder, *Acquisitions: where, what and how: a guide to orientation and procedure for students in librarianship, librarians, and academic faculty.* Westport, Conn.: Greenwood Press, 1978. p. 5.

FURTHER READING

Bremner, Joe and Peggy Miller. *Guide to Database Distribution: Legal Aspects and Model Contracts.* Philadelphia, PA: National Federation of Abstracting and Information Services, 1987. p .93.

"CD-ROM and the Law," *Microsoft CD-ROM Yearbook* 1989-1990. Redmond, WA: Microsoft Press, 1989. pp. 423-457.

Everett, John H. "Independent Information Professionals and the Question of Malpractice Liability," *Online* 13:3 (May 1989). pp. 65-70.

Galvin, Thomas J. and Sally Mason, eds. "Video, libraries and the law: Finding the balance," *American Libraries*, 20:2 (February 1989). pp. 110-119.

McKirdy, Pamela Reekes. "Copyright Issues for Microcomputer Collections," in *The Library Microcomputer Environment: Management Issues* by Sheila S. Intner and Jane Anne Hannigan. Phoenix, AZ: Oryx Press, 1988. pp. 96-125.

Journeymen of the Printing Office

Suzanne Freeman
Barbara A. Winters

SUMMARY. This article discusses the ethical and fiscal problems involved in the process of selecting and acquiring library materials in the current publishing climate. The authors address the impact of a number of factors, including the academic award system, on the publishing market and resulting issues to be addressed in the purchase of monographs and serials. Librarians' contributions to the publishing machine are briefly discussed. Possible solutions are outlined. A significant review of the literature is included; discussions of the problem can be found in the literature on publishing, written almost exclusively by professional writers, editors, or publishers. Librarians are just now beginning to comment.

With the greatest possible solicitude avoid authorship. Too early or immoderately employed, it makes the head waste and the heart empty, even were there no other worse consequences. A person who reads only to print in all probability reads amiss, and he who sends away through the pen and the press every thought the moment it occurs to him, will in a short time have sent all away, and will become a mere journeyman of the printing-office, a compositor.[1]

With publishing as the core of the academic award system, the establishment of claims to research and the building of a healthy publishing vita are paramount for those who seek promotion and tenure. The view that publication is synonymous with scholarship

Suzanne Freeman is Collection Management Librarian for Arts and Humanities and Barbara A. Winters is Head, Acquisition Services Department, with the Virginia Commonwealth University Library Services, 901 Park Avenue, Richmond, VA 23284-2033.

has gathered momentum since the early 1970s, causing a flood of journal articles and monographs on every conceivable aspect of nearly any given topic. At the same time, there has been an explosion in trade publishing as well, with over 7,500 works of fiction appearing in 1988 alone.[2] Significant discussions of this situation can be found in the literature on publishing, written almost exclusively by professional writers, editors, or publishers. With few exceptions, librarians have not commented on the sea of publications in which we find ourselves awash.[3]

This article will discuss the ethical and fiscal problems involved in the process of selecting and acquiring monographs and serials in the current publishing climate, and will examine librarians' contribution as professionals to the publishing "machine" as well as the possible solutions that might be employed.

SERIALS

Perhaps of greatest concern to those who select and procure materials are serials acquisitions. By their ongoing nature, they represent not only recurring costs that may skyrocket from one fiscal year to the next, but also publications whose frequency requires that blank pages be filled to meet strict deadlines in order for the title to continue to appear on schedule. When the need for "filler" arises, the material at hand may not be of the same quality as the rest of the issue. In addition, serial time constraints must surely make the author's temptation to pursue a topic of less complexity or resonance all the harder to resist.[4]

To complicate the selection process further, the splintering of certain disciplines and the resulting narrowness of focus are reflected in the growth of highly specialized journals, many of which are spin-offs from a more comprehensive parent title. Therefore, in order to provide the most complete coverage possible of a discipline, one now must consider the acquisition of multiple titles at a greater cost, with an eye toward possible overlapping of content with the original journal. For example, the ZEITSCHRIFT FUR PHYSIK, once one of the most inclusive journals in the field of physics, has spawned the following titles: PART A.: ATOMS AND NUCLEI (which subsequently splits into A. ATOMIC NUCLEI

and PART D.: ATOMS, MOLECULES, AND CLUSTERS);
PART B. CONDENSED MATTER AND QUANTA; and PART
C.: PARTICLES AND FIELDS. Undeniably, such specialization
may be warranted in many fields, but the attendant price tag for the
purchasing library may be prohibitive. The flow of ideas cannot be
stopped; however, the flow of information may need to be checked:

> . . . the multiplicity of journals results in a scattering of papers
> which makes it impossible for the scientist to keep informed of
> new developments, impossible for libraries to cover a field
> completely, . . . One writer estimates that a single article in a
> highly specialized periodical is of interest to only 10 percent of
> the workers in the subject area covered by the journal. . . . A
> scientist subscribing to a journal is forced to pay for twenty or
> thirty papers which do not concern him in order to get the one
> paper he wants.[5] (UNESCO)

It is interesting that, just as UNESCO estimates that any article
published is of interest to only 10% of the people in the field, some
scholars estimate that only 10% of publication is real scholarship.[6]
In addition, at least in the area of sociological research, it is thought
that few papers (even among those published in the most prestigious
journals) have had an impact on subsequent research.[7] Even in the
physical sciences, this has been thought to be the case. In 1963,
Thomas Kuhn put forth an argument that individual scientific discoveries are not bricks in the wall of the body of knowledge but that
all researchers work within certain paradigms; discoveries fit into
existing paradigms. From time to time new facts that cannot fit into
an existing paradigm appear and then a new paradigm must be con-
ceived.[8] If the Kuhn model represents the real relationship of pieces
of knowledge, the question that must be addressed by publishers
and librarians alike is how scientific information is communicated
within the paradigm, or perhaps how the communication facilitates
the construction of a new paradigm.

Selectors would do well to ask themselves just how many journals covering the same topic are really necessary, and they should
be particularly cautious if multiple journals on one topic are issued
by the same publisher. Even if the discipline boasts an energy spe-

cialist at the home institution, it is highly unlikely that three titles on heat and mass transfer would be needed to provide support for research and instruction. Indeed, a check of SCIENCE CITATION INDEX shows that only one of the titles in the field — largely self-citing — has a significant impact factor, while one of the remaining two is not even indexed. In a similar vein, one should seriously examine the content or coverage of journal titles produced by university departments or schools. The perceived prestige gained by the university through the publication of these titles may have little relation to the actual quality of the product or to the uniqueness of the knowledge that they transmit.[9]

Although core scholarly journals continue to be refereed, it appears that this no longer automatically insures them from the dangers of plagiarism or falsified information if recent instances of these abuses in medicine and the sciences can be taken as symptomatic.[10] A recent study of the disintegration of peer review suggests that the reasons for this are precisely those that are affecting the quality and quantity of material published.[11] The proliferation of publishing arenas and the concomitant increase in demand for material have made impractical the sort of rigorous and time-consuming review process that one expects to precede scholarly publication. The fragmenting of many disciplines also contributes to a weakening of the referee system: the more highly specialized the topic, the smaller the field of those who are actually qualified to comment and the greater the likelihood that "insular back-scratching among specialists"[12] may occur. The arrival of electronic publishing has enormous implications for the integrity and value of this material. If texts are transmitted without undergoing a formal process of publication, there will naturally be no opportunity for any sort of revision or review, impartial or not.

In disciplines like creative writing, new journals now often bloom and fade within a year, leaving the selector with the perplexing problem of weeding out those least likely to survive from the publishing year's latest crop. In most cases, traditional means of discerning quality in an unrefereed journal are useless. The presses are as new as the title that they are producing and therefore cannot be judged by their reputation. Nor can these journals be assessed by where they are indexed or cited because of their newness. Often the only course that remains is to run a check on the individual contributing authors in the hope that their previous publications will give some idea of the worth of their output – a procedure that can be expensive and extraordinarily time-consuming.

Managing the budget can become a juggling act. There is a decline in purchasing power resulting from the fluctuating strength or weakness of the U.S. dollar, inflation of costs per title, and the increase in the sheer amount of information published as cited above. A number of libraries are currently undergoing regular serials cancellation reviews to achieve a balance between journal and monograph expenditures, or are at the least requesting that an existing subscription of equal or greater value be cancelled before a new journal order is placed.

MONOGRAPHS

Two camps seem to exist in the book publishing trade: One camp decries the fact that fewer titles are being published at more cost per title. The other (represented by such critics as Arthur Krystal) is concerned over the perceived reality of a literary glut. As early as 1819, Washington Irving was brooding: "The stream of literature has swollen into a torrent – augmented into a river – expanded into a sea. . . . It will soon be the employment of a lifetime merely to learn [books'] names. Many a man of passable information at the present day reads scarcely anything but reviews, and before long, a man of erudition will be little better than a mere walking catalog."[13] *Publisher's Weekly* book title output figures validate the latter concern. The Editor-in-Chief of *PW* declared in 1987 that publishers were metamorphosing into snake-oil salesmen, making thoughtless publishing decisions (which were neither wise nor ethical), and were guilty of publishing superstitious nonsense as if it were serious scientific theory.[14]

Responsible procurement of monographs has, then, become increasingly difficult, given the current climate in the academic and publishing worlds. Aside from the staggering quantity that one must face – over 50,000 titles published in a single year[15] – is the task of ascertaining the quality of these works.

The fact that the author is well-known is often the selector's only reliable rule-of-thumb. Both trade and university presses are publishing what Frederick A. Hetzel has called the "Competent Manuscript," which often requires significant revision before publication.[16] Worse still are those manuscripts that appear in print without the necessary editorial attention. Highly specific dissertation topics that would be better served if published as one or more journal articles appear instead as monographs whose length may testify more to the author's stamina for research than to the actual quality of the finished work.[17]

The fragmentation of disciplines mentioned earlier is but one of the factors that governs the academic authors' choice of monographic topics, dictating an approach that must be narrow in order to appeal to their small and specialized audience. In the humanities, this specialization is the result of the dearth of new frontiers to be explored from a broad perspective. Authors may thus be left with a choice between singling out a finite portion of their area of interest for prolonged examination, or discovering a new angle from which to rewrite what has already been done. This is not to suggest that these works are not "Competent Manuscripts," but to ask if what they are addressing adds enough substance to the body of knowledge in their discipline to warrant acquisition, given the straitened budgetary circumstances within which we must select.

If one happens to have a book in hand, through an approval plan or through other means, the selection process becomes less of a guessing game. Primary sources with no preface or editing, works with no substantial index, and "cocktail table" art books are easily identified. Authors' credentials or previously acclaimed publications are usually revealed on the dust jacket or on the title page.

Unfortunately, the bulk of the publishing universe that we must monitor is usually accessible only through title announcements, reviews, or publishers' blurbs, of which the latter two should be taken with a large pinch of salt by the selector. Even the most reliable reviewing sources may contain assessments that are less than thorough or that reflect a strong bias on the part of the reviewer. Other reviews may be even more misleading in their prescriptive stance, recommending a different title for acquisition rather than addressing whether or not the work in question covers the author's stated thesis. Most egregious is the hype that can accompany new trade monographs, where the success of the titles is often linked to a sensationalism that obscures the quality, or lack thereof, of the new publications and equates those authors who may be truly outstanding with those who are merely notorious.

As is the case with journals, the peer review system for monographs that we associate with scholarly publishing may no longer be the guarantee of quality that one used to expect.

ACCESS

In many emerging organizational models, acquisitions librarians are directly responsible for access to materials. In all models, they are indirectly responsible. At the same time, the expansion of our knowledge base is now legendary, as described above.

The number of journals abstracted by Chemical Abstracts Service increased by over 1000% from 1927 (when the totality of chemical literature was abstracted) to 1976 (when CAS was not scratching the surface of what was available).[18]

There exists, then, both an ethical and fiscal dilemma for the librarian: how to keep the various literatures current enough to support patron needs without becoming captive to the publishing machine. Further, entirely new ethical discussions about the self-limiting possibilities of access vs. ownership (via online fulltext databases), limiting access only to the elite (or those who can pay), are resurfacing.

Networking (with the potential of providing more equitable access) is something librarians have talked about for a number of years but have not yet been successful in implementing, except through conventional interlibrary loan processes. In fact, a number of multi-branch libraries can scarcely network with their own branches, let alone with a state, local, or national system. Cooperative collection development, providing access and not necessarily ownership, will be a necessity – not just a buzz phrase – in the near future.

POSSIBLE SOLUTIONS

What can the solution be to this dilemma? At this point in history, no one has *the* solution but a number of mini-solutions may be presented:

1. Librarians must become partners with publishers. Marcia Tuttle, for one, believes that such a partnership now appears possible.[19] Publishing *is* commerce, and what does not sell will not be published. We must rethink our collection priorities and create and monitor our own price indexes. In the past, librarians have been able to have some effect on their plight; for example, a few years ago, librarians uncovered discriminatory pricing to the U.S. market of foreign journals through observation of pricing patterns and turned the situation around. We must constantly monitor and periodically revisit such practices.

2. We can re-examine the access vs. ownership issue afresh and look for solutions as yet untried. One example is the CD-ROM-publishing marketplace. The trial ADONIS project, for instance, is a document delivery service that supplies full-text, laser printed copies of articles appearing in 219 core biomedical journals (stored on CD-ROM). There are document distribution centers worldwide, including Information on Demand in Berkeley.[20] The Faxon Company allows access to ADONIS through the Infoserve function of its mainframe system. One concern about this particular project is that the original partners in the consortium that developed the ADONIS project are the very publishers that have already added to the library's plight by charging journal prices that provide comfortable profits. Again, this type of access is an ethical problem in itself, the long range result of which may be an increasing information "elitism," which is in need of the intervention and interpretation of library professionals. Richard Rowe may have the solution to this dilemma:

> Many forces are at work in bringing about the shift toward consumer-oriented knowledge. While we must go in that direction, we must also ensure a balance in the process. There are certain things we must do to foster this balance between hot and cool information.[21]

Rowe goes on to list six ways to guarantee the balance between free and fee-based access. Included are exhortations to clarify goals in an effort to strike a balance between investments and consumption, and to develop a form of "social audit" to measure how these goals are being met; to increase public awareness about the importance of investing resources in disciplines that have no immediate payoff, such as the arts and humanities; and to establish investment standards, including what sort of priority should be given to networking.

Librarians must become proactive in the electronic publishing arena. Our future as librarians may very well be tied to our ability to do so.[22] We must be prepared to disseminate formally-reviewed and revised research and scholarship electronically in the near future.

3. We can start at home by making a determination, as professionals, not to contribute unrefereed materials to the publishing machine, thus guaranteeing the preservation of the integrity of peer review relative to our own publications. We must contribute, not as slaves of the academic award system, but as professionals who have something of value to communicate. (In a subsequent article, the authors hope to survey the review and publishing practices of the major library journal publications.) In addition, we should heed the urging of Kenneth Eble, echoed in our own literature by John Lubans,[23] that assessment of our scholarship, or scholarly competence, not be based solely on a list of published works, but rather on a broad spectrum of professional activities that would represent new measures of quality. In this way, we might insure that what is published in librarianship is of the caliber that we demand from the monographs and serials that we select and acquire.

REFERENCES

1. Johann Gottfried Herder, in Samuel Taylor Coleridge. *Biographia Literaria*, ed. George Watson. (London: Dent, 1975), p. 133, footnote 3.
2. Arthur Krystal, "On Writing: Let There Be Less," *New York Times Book Review*, March 26, 1989, p. 23.
3. The authors were pleased to see that Richard Dougherty brought the crisis of journal costs to the attention of the academic community recently in a Point-of-View article for *The Chronicle of Higher Education*, wherein he recommended that universities re-assume the responsibility for publishing their own research

("To Meet the Crisis in Journal Costs, Universities Must Reassert Their Role in Scholarly Publishing," 35[1] [April 12, 1989] p. A52). John Lubans, Jr., published a cogent article dealing with the issues of "scholarly drivel" that appeared in *American Libraries* in March 1987. This was unsuccessfully rebutted in the September 1987 issue by Bert R. Boyce and Danny P. Wallace. Most recently Marcia Tuttle, in presenting a summary of the proceedings of the SSP Sixth Annual Top Management Roundtable, discusses the Society's focus on quality in scholarly communication ("Quality—It's Expensive—Can We Afford It?" *Library Acquisitions: Practice & Theory* 12 (1988) pp. 1-10).

4. Ernest Cadman Colwell, "The Publishing Needs of Scholarship." *Scholarly Publishing*, 6(2) (January 1975), pp. 102-103; Harris J. Bullford (pseud.), "Scaling the Ivory Tower." *Change*, 19(5) (September/October 1987): pp. 56-57.

5. Ralph H. Phelps and John P. Herlin. "Alternatives to the Scientific Periodical." *UNESCO Bulletin for Libraries* 14 (March-April 1960): p. 62.

6. F.E.L. Priestly, Harvey Kerpneck. "Publication and Academic Award." *Scholarly Publishing* 8(3) (April 1977): p. 234.

7. Mark Oromaner. "When Publications Perish." *Scholarly Publishing* 10(4) (July 1979): pp. 339-344.

8. Thomas S. Kuhn. *The Structure of Scientific Revolutions*. (Chicago: University of Chicago Press, 1962), 172 pp.

9. Colwell, p. 103.

10. Walter W. Stewart and Ned Feder. "The Integrity of the Scientific Literature." *Nature* 325 (January 15, 1987): pp. 207-214.

11. James M. Banner, Jr. "Preserving the Integrity of Peer Review." *Scholarly Publishing* 19(2) (January 1988): p. 109-115.

12. Banner, p. 109.

13. In Krystal, p. 23.

14. "Questionable Publishing Judgments." *Publishers Weekly* 232 (August 14, 1987): p. 12.

15. Krystal, p. 1.

16. Frederick A. Hetzel. "Publish or Perish, and the Competent Manuscript." *Scholarly Publishing* 4(2) (January 1973): p. 102.

17. John B. Putnam. "The Scholar and the Future of Scholarly Publishing." *Scholarly Publishing* 4(3) (April 1973): p. 199.

18. Richard Kaser, unpublished talk presented at the Society for Scholarly Publishing Future of Scholarly Journals Seminar, Chapel Hill, N.C., October 17-19, 1988, as reported by Deana L. Astle, "The Scholarly Journal, Whence or Whither," unpublished talk presented at the College of Charleston Conference on Issues in Book and Serial Acquisition, Charleston, S.C., November 4, 1988.

19. Tuttle, p. 10.

20. Constance Orchard. "ADONIS and Electronically Stored Information: An Information Broker's Experience" in *Serials Information from Publisher to User*. (New York: The Haworth Press, 1988): pp. 85-91.

21. Richard R. Rowe. "Cold Storage and Fast Food: The Feeding of Discovery." *The Serials Librarian* 15(1/2) (1988): pp. 5-16.

22. Arnold Hirshon presented an excellent paper on this topic at the ALA Acquisitions program in Dallas, Texas, on June 25, 1989. (The paper is soon to be published in an issue of *LRTS*.)

23. Lubans, p. 182.

24. Kenneth E. Eble. "Scholarly Publishing and Academic Reward." *Scholarly Publishing* 6(1) (October 1974): pp. 19-25.

Contracts and Ethics
in Library Acquisitions:
The Expressed and the Implied

James R. Coffey

SUMMARY. This article examines the legal and ethical bases of the business relationship between libraries and booksellers. It focuses the reader on the need for awareness of these factors as a means for measuring the quality of one's own work performance. The legal framework of interaction between the two is explained briefly and comment is made with regard to the lack of litigation. It discusses the implied adjustment of librarians' attention to the whole process rather than on the library's internal operations only. The ethics of competence is discussed and illustrated with a view to showing that librarians' strict control and awareness of the dynamics of the process will enable them to function on an equal footing in the marketplace.

INTRODUCTION

Before looking at the legal circumstances of our relationship with suppliers and our ethical response to them, let us try taking our moral temperature as de Tocqueville observed Americans are always doing. Is it normal? – and are we healthy? When was the last flagrant violation of ethics on the part of an acquisitions librarian reported in the news or along the grapevine? I don't remember hearing of one – nor do I think that if there were anything interesting to hear about, it would be widespread among the profession. So we are in good shape, right? Maybe not. We may be nice people who don't do bad things; but are we really nice people who don't do

---

James R. Coffey is Technical Services Librarian at Rutgers University, Camden campus, Camden, NJ 08102.

good things either? When did you last give a thought to giving yourself a performance rating on what you know about your job and how well you do it? Does the thought make you uneasy because there wouldn't be enough time for such (frivolous) exercises? — or because you are not sure of what you would include? — or does the thought just not make you uneasy?

Getting materials into the library is the *raison d'etre* of acquisitions and from the day we take over, our activities revolve around that goal. Reflecting on that activity as something having a legal or ethical basis may not have occurred to us as a worthwhile or even appropriate thing to do. We are not lawyers nor do we feel comfortable as guardians of virtue. So why pursue such a line of inquiry? Why take the time to be philosophical, an expendable exercise for busy people. We should pursue it because we may find that we had forgotten an important element of functioning well or that we had not quite understood it so clearly before. We may find that keeping the legal and ethical in mind could give us more confidence in what we do and sure guidelines for how to do it. It could provide a measuring device with which to make judgments about how to go about the business of acquisitions. We should pursue it also because there *are* legal and ethical influences at work in the environment of library acquisitions and, with a heightened awareness of them, we may not be so quick to give ourselves a good rating for performing well. This article will demonstrate hopefully the need to make sure that legality and ethics function routinely and consciously as part of the acquisitions librarian's view of the job and that they guide the process toward efficiency and competence.

In order to do this, we will consider first a general view of the dynamics of the library/supplier relationship, then the legal framework, and finally the ethical circumstances. At the end of this article, it should be evident that it is worth the time and attention to reflect on these aspects of our jobs.

The focus of this paper will be on what is the legal and ethical environment of acquisitions and on what is the nature of the relationship. The emphasis will be on the librarian. Are we doing well in our awareness of how these aspects of our job affect our performance? — or is there something to be learned? Let us look first and quickly to a description of the simple dynamics of the relationship for an idea of how libraries and suppliers can interact.

THE ACQUISITIONS LIBRARIAN

When the acquisitions librarian sends an order to a supplier, he or she places the library into a contractual process the expectations of which are often clearly understood by the principals involved: the supply of materials quickly and accurately. The librarian, in view of the institutional expectations placed on acquisitions, usually emphasizes the timely delivery of the materials requested and tends to evaluate a supplier, among other things, in terms of the shortness of time in which a quantity of items is delivered. Except when the supplier is totally unsuitable to the library's needs, most of the materials probably arrive within a reasonable time to the requestor and don't give rise to comment or cause problems. The defects of this system of supply, however, are often seen in the dramatic failure to supply bibliographer A or professor B with something expected. Less often, but perhaps more reliably, these defects are demonstrated by vendor studies which show quantitatively what has not been delivered within a given range of purchase orders.

Vendor performance generates a great deal of discussion in acquisitions departments and at meetings; and acquisitions librarians and their departments generate a great deal of discussion among vendors. Frustration is often the common thread—plenty of heat but often not very much light. Part of the frustration is caused by a lack of familiarity with the operational workflow or with the constraints and demands made on one or the other of the parties; and until that is made clear, the frustrations may continue. This state of affairs could, with effort, be changed and not go on indefinitely; and an understanding may be reached between the two. To begin with, an awareness of the legal, commercial, and ethical context of the library/supplier relationship, by making clear the bases of the relationship, would give the acquisitions librarian a more secure grasp not only of his or her own operation, but also that of the supplier and, more remotely, that of the publisher. In addition, it may give a surer sense of how to acquire materials faster and cheaper. As I hope to show later, these bases are often obscure even when they are actually recognized and understood.

THE LEGAL PERSPECTIVE

To explore this, let us look at some points of commercial law and acquire thereby some idea of the contractual aspect of our jobs as acquisitions librarians.[1]

To get an idea of the legal context, we should be aware of how the library/supplier relationship is determined contractually, what regulates it, what factors are considered in forming and disputing a contract, how the parties are protected, what kind of contract it is, what makes the formation of the contract clear, what is its duration, and how it is validated. A great deal can be said by way of illustrating these factors; but I will confine myself to a few essential points because the legal realities are basically simple.

The process itself comes down to a short formula: supply and pay. The supplier undertakes to get materials into the library and the library undertakes to pay for them. The faster this takes place, the closer we come to the ideal. The following paragraphs will show how we arrive at this formula.

It is perhaps most accurate to view the contract between library and supplier as a process (or a continuous stream of processes) in which the library offers to pay the vendor who offers to supply a quantity of materials at a reasonable price within a reasonable frame of time. Although the supply of library materials is not strictly comparable to the supply of automobiles, furniture, etc., with which most litigation is familiar, and although the partial and gradual nature of delivery is also not usual, the process itself is still not so unique with regard to contracts as to constitute special handling in the courts. Accordingly, it is covered by the Uniform Commercial Code which has been adopted by most states and territories (except Louisiana and Puerto Rico) which in turn have added many non-uniform amendments. The code itself, in regard to sale of goods, is supplemented by case law and the Restatement (Second) of 1981 which functions as a persuasive authority. The latter two are resorted to conventionally when the UCC does not cover the issue at hand. To the extent that the Code *is* relevant to the case under consideration, it must be applied. In litigation, the process would also be susceptible to "reasonable interpretation" of the terms and circumstances involved which, in fact, would mean that a court would view any disputes in the light of how much the case in hand were to represent a departure from normal, conventional occurrences in this type of business.

In addition, the contract would have to entail "good faith, diligence, or care" on the part of both parties. There cannot be any hidden advantage to one party to the extraordinary disadvantage of the other. The acquisitions process, therefore, is protected in law by means of the Code, the amendments, the Restatement, reasonable interpretation, conventional business practice, and recognition of dealing in good faith. The ample protection afforded by law prevents contracts contrary to its provisions from being formed, attempts to avoid harm to both parties, and attempts to keep the unwitting from being taken advantage of. It is important to keep in mind however that, while the law intends to keep the process fair and reasonable to both sides, the ideal is to avoid becoming entangled in litigation. To do this, the librarian has to be alert to what is going on in the business relationship. In a recent article on contracts for library systems, David Genaway made the observation that "As a consumer, the best defense against ending up with a bad contract is a good offense in the selection and planning stages."[2]

Several other considerations should be mentioned in order to view the context within which we operate. One is that the contract is bilateral: a promise for a promise. The library promises to pay; the supplier promises to deliver. Both must signal clearly the intention to contract and the library usually does this by sending single or list purchase orders for materials. The intent of the contractual process is clear (the supply of materials) and, unless accompanied by a letter stating otherwise or by verbal negotiations, unambiguous. An example of ambiguity might be a request for price quotes which was interpreted as an order to supply. Most of the time, however, sending purchase orders is clear evidence of intent.

When there is a dispute as to whether a contract was ever intended, the courts tend to favor formation of contract, if the context suggests it and if a "reasonable" third-party interpretation would support it. Not all the material terms have to be included either.

The duration of the contract is usually held to be until the contract is cancelled for a good reason and within a reasonable period of time. A cancellation on its way to the supplier while the book is in transit cannot be honored; or, on the other hand, if publication has been cancelled, then an order cannot be expected to be left outstanding. Technically, however, a book which becomes available five years after the date of order (at eight times the original price of $65.00) and without a specific understanding of "quotes before sending," may be supplied to the library with expectation of payment. A bookseller, however, often informs the requestor before sending. Time of performance, on the other hand, relates to how long it may take a supplier to deliver. In the "fill or kill" context (i.e., a directive to the dealer to supply from the dealer's stock only and to cancel otherwise), time of performance and duration of contract are the same. Since libraries order a number of items at one time and since they will be delivered at varying times, the duration of contract and time of performance are usually left open with the expectation that it will be "reasonable."

The contractual process requires the consent of both parties (offer and acceptance) and the library usually begins the process by sending out an order or orders. The library can provide (but seldom does) that the acceptance be effective only when the materials are delivered. Failing this stipulation, the law generally interprets the acceptance to be effective once the materials are placed in the mail by the supplier.

The legal process now requires validation of the contract. The offer and acceptance may have been made but may not be legally enforceable. The validation is by "bargained-for" consideration; i.e., a clear recognition of what each stands to gain and what each has to give up (benefit and detriment). Some contractual statements include a statement of consideration (for, and in consideration of . . .); but the point is that there must be a give and take on both sides, that the contract allows for presuming a reasonable relationship between the benefit to the promisor and the detriment to the promisee. Consideration used to be evidenced by means of a seal; but this has been replaced by evidence of benefit and detriment.

The foregoing considerations give us some perspective on the legal circumstances of the library/vendor relationship—but to what extent do they have any effect on the actual daily operation of library acquisitions? No one ever seems to hear much about legal battles between libraries and suppliers — at least not ones that shake acquisitions departments to the foundations. This tranquility, however, is probably no accident. Looked at from one point of view, there is no litigation because everything is working perfectly. From the legal standpoint, this is probably so: libraries and suppliers identify their needs and expectations clearly; they both stand to gain from the relationship; they are both competent to contract; their activities are sanctioned by law; they are free to act; and performance is adequate according to conventional business practice. If pushed, we could probably find something over which to confront each other in court, but we don't, partly because the stakes are not high enough to be worth it. In a court, the process would probably be judged to be working well anyway.

But we do have problems with the way each party performs and we all have a lot to say about it. It is not worth going to court over our mutual performance in this contractual process, but it is this area which generates the controversy. Many studies have been done to show how well vendors (specifically named) supply books: the rate of supply, the number, the numbers not supplied, etc. No vendor, on the other hand, has published studies on how well libraries pay for the materials. You may find out years after the fact that your institution took longer than any other to pay a national vendor located in your own town.

It may be prudent of a supplier to act as if the customer is always right and to suggest gingerly to a library that payments are outstanding; but the legal obligation is to supply and pay — and while the supplier may give evidence of many defects in sending materials, we have to recognize that fair behavior requires us to pay in a timely manner. Since there is no flagrant breach of contract (or not any breach that would be improved by litigation), libraries and suppliers will not take each other into court and will probably continue in a relationship that is not wholly satisfying. The process does work enough of the time to stay viable and, although we could pay less for it, there is no cost-effective alternative.

From the legal standpoint then, libraries are getting what is contracted for and what might be called for would be a sharpening of standards on both sides of the supply-and-pay equation. What we are asking for legally in this process becomes obscured by our internal needs, pressures from outside the library's acquisitions department, and by conveniences. In negotiations between library and vendor, the focus often shifts unconsciously to the wish list agenda of the sales representative and the acquisitions librarian. "I will supply X, if you will pay Y" becomes taken for granted and replaced by "If you send all your (good) orders to us, I will invoice by purchase order number, fund number, and main entry (whatever that is), package alphabetically by title, gift wrap staff orders, deliver by UPS at 20% discount across the board and no postage." Such negotiations are not unheard of. One can anchor oneself back in reality by remembering that if the vendor throws each book through the library window, the contract would probably be upheld as long as the invoice is thrown in along with them. The process tends to become strained by unrealistic hopes and expectations. Even if the library did send $500,000 worth of (good) orders, what is gained if payment is not received for six to nine months? The vendor can no longer borrow against the receivables and interest is being paid on what has been borrowed. With the above-mentioned (admittedly extreme) example, the librarian would have to realize that any such demands take time and slow down the shipment, cost money (because now people would have to do more to prepare it for shipping), and result in higher prices. So what looks like the best deal or most convenient arrangement for the library can turn to its disadvantage in the long run.

If we keep the legal perspective in mind, we can make better-informed judgments about the process and tailor our expectations to our performance. We will let the process do what it is intended to do. We will not make excessive demands on it, and we will see better results.

THE ETHICAL PERSPECTIVE

It is in the area of ethics that the dramas of library/supplier relationships have meaning and come into relief because that is where the real issues arise. This is the area over which we have personal control and where we have latitude for determining what is going to be done. There is generally no mechanism, however, for self-checking to see whether we have behaved appropriately. For vendors, sales call reports provide a measuring device for the sales representative. Such devices don't exist for librarians and no third party is ever asked to comment on the process or to evaluate how well the librarian has represented the institution or how well the institution has lived up to its side of the contract.

If the acquisitions librarian is conscious of ethical standards in the relationship, then there is an impulse to explore the means to clarifying misunderstandings, to discriminate with regard to the respective responsibilities of the parties involved and thereby to avoid the conflict. By ethics I am not referring to the opportunities for personal gain at the expense of the system. This type of concern has been getting appropriate attention in the recent literature. I am concerned instead with the ethics of competence which might sound like a novelty but which is not new. One of the recurrent themes enunciated by the American Library Association in statements on professional ethics deals with competence. A professional librarian is expected to be competent in handling professional responsibilities. "Librarians are dependent upon one another for the bibliographical resources that enable us to provide information services, and have obligations for maintaining the highest level of personal integrity and competence."[3]

If one is to function as an acquisitions librarian, then it seems fair to expect that person to be informed. Being informed about acquisitions librarianship is largely a matter of chance since no provision is made in the library schools for preparing people for it. Management of work, personnel supervision, the mechanics of publishing and bookselling, commercial law, or ethics don't seem to receive much attention in library schools and, given that fact, the achievements of librarians, who are often self-trained, are spectacular. However, that is not enough. Competence requires a full knowledge of the conditions of doing business—for publishers and suppliers as well as for libraries—including workflow organization, its rationale, and the ins and outs of publisher/vendor relationships. A thorough grasp of these areas will give the librarian a basis for informed judgment which is what is needed to prevent the misunderstandings which arise among us. This lack of the complete picture and of appreciation of the other's milieu leads to a waste of time, money, and energy some of which could be focused on the realities of the marketplace over the next few years. John Secor, in an article on business ethics refers to three areas of concern for the near future:

1. The necessary transition into the information age.
2. The globalization and conglomeration of publishing and vending, with resulting manage for survival or manage for success mindsets.
3. The need for librarians to develop reasonable (business-oriented) expectations relating to vendor services — recognizing that publishers, library booksellers, and periodical vendors must receive fair compensation for their creative labor.[4]

Making up for the lack in professional school preparation is the acquisitions librarian's responsibility. Managing large sums of money and labor-intensive operations (however well justified) will not be left forever in the hands of the acquisitions librarian alone if the resource crisis continues to focus the attention of directors on ways to cut down. Greater competence is worth the effort because it, among other things, gives the librarian the power to stand on an equal business footing with the publisher and vendor when it comes to restructuring the economic environment of acquisitions over the next decade. It is to be hoped that the librarian will not need to rely on trust alone to get a good deal and to be an equal partner in the triangular relationship.

It is rare to catch the library/vendor relationship in an unguarded moment — one in which feelings of mistrust are aired in a public forum. In 1984, however, this did happen and the incident is worth quoting in full:

* * *

ALA Ethics Committee looks at vendor-library relationships

Judging by the interplay between vendors and librarians at the meeting of ALA's Professional Ethics Committee in Dallas, many, but not all, have come a long way from the days when they eyed each other with fear and loathing.

Pat Barkalow, a former librarian and now a GEAC staffer, provided a tongue-in-cheek analysis of the "expectations" of librarians: that public librarians are service-centered, dedicated to free access to information, innocent, and pure in spirit. Academic librarians, on the other hand, see themselves as great ammassers and protectors of knowledge, with the sacred duty to buy one of everything published.

In general, she said, librarians see serials vendors as greedy, maybe a little corrupt, needing watching. Automation vendors, operating under the mystique of computers, can be saviors and problem solvers — or charlatans taking advantage of the librarian's lack of understanding of automation. Greed, not altruism, is seen to motivate them.

"Vendors, on the other hand, *have* to be service oriented or they're out of business," said Barkalow. Meanwhile, librarians can no longer hide behind their service-centered image; today they have to justify their existence and even become profit-centered and work at bringing in funds.

Images, then, are changing for both librarians and vendors. Trust between them was undermined first by the failure and withdrawal from the market of a couple of big vendors. A vendor can be driven out of business by what librarians say about him.

But today both librarians and vendors recognize that theirs is a symbiotic relationship, where each has the welfare of the other in keeping.

Librarians were assailed for putting price before quality and for buying pirated films by a representative of one film vendor. "Dealers do entice, seduce, but the responsibility to say yes or no is yours," she said, going on to damn librarians for a new ethical sin, racism, blaming them for the unwillingness of vendors to hire blacks as sales people.

Vendors, on the other hand, often "won't take a drink unless the librarian does, and won't make unethical proposals unless the librarian hints that they will be welcome." The tirade ended with, "I doubt that more than ten percent of you will be affected by what I say."

"An arms-length relationship is the best," said another vendor rep. Improper inducements, on the other hand, lead to a lack of trust, higher prices, and poorer service.

It was left for Donald Satisky (Blackwell/North America) to find mellow words to bring peace at the end. Pointing out that the customer-salesman relationship often becomes a client relationship and often leads to real friendships. Satisky said vendor hospitality suites rarely involve business discussions and the vendors frequently don't even know many of the people who show up. He said that with the increasing number of librarians on vendor staffs, many are having more difficulty deciding whether they are for "them" or "us."[5]

*   *   *

A lot could be read between the lines here and, although the waters were calmed, the issues have not been resolved. For one thing, the emotions did not obscure the fact that each side does not have much experience or knowledge of the other's work environment. Vendors often hire librarians to represent them; but these librarians don't always have experience in acquisitions so the fact that they are librarians may be irrelevant. The mistrust is founded basically on ignorance or indifference but it is fortified by personal experiences of unethical or incompetent behavior on the part of individuals and sometimes generalized to be universal. Griping is often the result; but this is unproductive and it won't help in the 1990's when the prospects of shrinking resources and lower discounts will loom larger.

Examples can be helpful in focusing attention on principles (or points of departure). The following may serve to illustrate better some of the ideas expressed above. None of the following examples is based on imagination; but each is a composite of personal experiences either in customer services or in sales.

1. A sales representative of a vendor has arranged to visit a librarian with a view to getting that librarian to buy books from the sales representative's company. He or she, in addition to a basic salary which is not as high as people imagine, works on a commission basis and depends first on making a reasonable number of sales calls and then on spending time wisely. Volume of sales is impor-

tant and therefore high on the list of priorities in persuading a potential customer to do business.

There are two ethical pitfalls potential to this scenario. One is that the representative will listen to the expressed needs of the librarian, and in order to get the business, offer to meet those needs, without regard to the ability of the company to follow through. The priority here seems to be the personal bottom line for the sales representative. The other possibility is that the librarian, who has no intention of doing business with this company (and may have said so), will take up valuable time in a lengthy interview. The priority here is that someone else's bottom line is not something to worry about.

2. The director of a community college library is telling a sales representative about the difficulties of acquiring materials for the library and the amount of work that goes into doing so. The acquisitions librarian is working very hard and they have been told to take advantage of every opportunity to get discounts. Their approach has been to send every order to a nearby bookseller who gives good discounts. This assures them the advantage of high discount on books which actually entail a discount. Whatever is not supplied in four months is cancelled and ordered directly. This comes to about 40% of the library's orders. Some of these 40% can be acquired from another vendor at a lower discount but many of them carry no discount at all and would cost the supplier a few dollars per item to supply: handbooks for local volunteer firefighters; guides to flower arranging techniques by the Millenarian Horticultural Society; transparencies for training bus drivers for local retirement communities, etc. The acquisitions librarian has doubts about the sincerity of dealers who claim they will supply this kind of material and thinks that there may be a better way to do business. There is a real need to have these materials and they are ultimately ordered directly. Even so they have to send claims or call sometimes before the material comes in. Sometimes the publishers actually reply long after the library could have used the material.

Notwithstanding the efforts of the people involved to do the best they can, there is here clearly an issue of competence. The librarians should be thinking of how much it costs to process invoices for single items, of whether suppliers could be used more effectively even with service charges, of what it costs to redirect orders, and of what it costs to order directly. Above all the librarian should be able to recognize that not all orders are alike, that the library has a broad mix of orders and that its operations require a special approach in order to maximize efficiency. It should be clear that what the library is doing is not effective and needs to be changed. The library could continue to use their primary dealer because it is to its real advantage to do so for a large number of its orders; but the library could do so with a better understanding of what that dealer can supply. The library could also use the "fair mix" concept to good effect with other dealers. It seems to me that someone who is a director of a library ought to have a better grasp of what is involved in the ordering process.

3. A library system has just negotiated an agreement with a bookseller to provide books at an advantageous discount based on the volume of business the bookseller anticipates over the course of each fiscal year. The library is especially pleased with having an easy method of monitoring the vendor's performance with regard to discount and has made it clear that it will stop doing business if all the terms are not complied with.

It is easy to note that the vendor could do a number of things to avoid a total commitment to the terms of the agreement: not ordering the low discount items and reporting them unavailable, raising the list price before discounting, etc. However, dealers negotiate these agreements without knowing any more than the library just exactly what kinds of orders will be placed over the next six to twelve months; so no one can be sure of how profitable the mix will be and whether it will justify the negotiated discount. Dealers make educated guesses based on the buying patterns of the past, the descriptions of the libraries' needs, the size of the budget, the kinds of books which comparable libraries buy and a number of other factors which enable them to predict reasonably what profit there will be. If a vendor is not careful about this, it may face the prospect of going out of business.

For the library, the issue in this case is the degree to which it is able to monitor its own performance. A dealer will watch the account and see very quickly whether the anticipated type of order is being placed; but what would the library do? One easy thing to do would be to send everything to the dealer; but that has its disadvantages as has been seen in the past. Another would be to wait until the dealer calls to say the library has to change its ordering pattern. It is not always easy to predict the library's reaction to that kind of communication even though it has to be done. The library would have to devise some method for analysing its order mix according to how the books will be discounted by the publisher and, like the dealer, be prepared for some surprises. Publishers don't always discount according to what is anticipated. The point, in this case, is that competence requires the library to have its own, sure method of checking on compliance. Otherwise it has all the power over the arrangement and no answerability.

4. An acquisitions librarian makes an appointment to see the sales representative of a regional bookseller. The sales representative looks forward to the opportunity to introduce this large, public library to his company and to get a share of the business. At the beginning of the interview the librarian, who does not have a lot of time this morning, is quick to apologize for the necessary brevity but says he wanted very much to be able to talk. He goes on to say how much he has enjoyed dealing with his company in the past, has been satisfied with the delivery and reporting and has no complaints. Then he changes the subject and goes on at great length about having to operate acquisitions in a warehouse facility sixteen blocks from the library and how difficult it is to get from one place to the other. Suddenly, he looks at his watch and apologizes about having to terminate the interview to go to a meeting. He concludes by saying that he looks forward to seeing the sales representative again sometime during the next year. As he leaves, he asks for the sales representative's card, looks at it for a minute and then thanks him for coming.

These examples do not illustrate that librarians are unethical or incompetent necessarily, but they do suggest that there is sometimes a serious lack in what is needed to function well as informed, professional people who are to be taken seriously, especially by people who come from profit-oriented environments in which accountability is an integral part of keeping a job.

CONCLUSION

I would like to suggest that the ideal environment would entail a recognition of the fact that the dealer must supply materials, all or most of them, fast and unencumbered by special arrangements or unrealistic expectations regarding discounts and service charges. We, in turn, would pay promptly—pay before reconciling the invoice, if necessary. We do this essentially for deposit accounts. Acquisitions librarians would organize their workflows to avoid cost-consuming routines. They would know what it takes to get a book from the mind of an author to the receiving department of a library and how this is done. They would work toward operational routines which would keep down the costs for everyone. They would take responsibility for their own internal processes and not let the vendor shoulder any such responsibilities. They would keep a sharp eye on their own standards of ethics, not being open to preposterous offers nor expecting what is unrealistic through ignorance. They would recognize, because of their own knowledge, whether the library is being dealt with fairly and not rely so heavily on the element of "trust." As aware and competent librarians, this is the least we can expect of ourselves.

Emerging from the 1990's is going to take more than trust. Getting into and through them will take a good sense of business—and being fully cognizant of the process is our ethical responsibility as librarians.

REFERENCES

1. Corley, Robert N., Eric M. Holmes, and William J. Robert. *Principles of Business Law*. 12th ed. Englewood Cliffs, Prentice-Hall, 1983: 185-348.
2. Genaway, David C. "Contracts: ironclad paper tigers." *Technicalities* 8 (August, 1988): 8-10.
3. "Statement on Professional Ethics 1981: Introduction." *American Libraries* June, 1981: 335.
4. Secor, John R. "A Growing Crisis of Business Ethics: the Gathering Stormclouds." *The Serials Librarian* 13 (Oct/Nov.—1987): 67-84.
5. "ALA Ethics Committee looks at vendor-library relationships." *Library Journal* September 1, 1984: 1584-1586.

Obscenity and Juveniles:
A Look at Commonwealth v.
American Booksellers

Bruce Strauch

SUMMARY. This article presents a detailed view of one legal case regarding obscene materials and the First Amendment guarantees of free speech. Implications for juvenile access to this type of material are discussed. In addition, further reading is cited.

Libraries have all variety of users, even college and university libraries which are used primarily by consenting adults. However, obscenity statutes exist in most states which can call into question the fact that some libraries, being public places, may contain materials which can be deemed harmful to juveniles, either from the nearby town or from the families of faculty, staff, and students, and the like. Do libraries have a legal obligation to ban these materials from this type of user group?

Though the obscenity statutes vary widely among the states, there is some recent legal precedent worth noting that arises from Virginia and the U.S. Supreme Court.

The First Amendment guarantees free speech and leaves to the people the right to evaluate ideas however pernicious. "If there is any fixed star in our constitutional constellation, it is that no official, high or petty, can prescribe what shall be orthodox in politics, nationalism, religion, or other matters of opinion or force citizens to confess by word or act their faith therein." *West Virginia State*

Bruce Strauch is Associate Professor with the Department of Business Administration, The Citadel, Charleston, SC 29409.

111

Board of Education v. Barnette, 319 U.S. 624, 642, 63 S.Ct. 1178, 1187, 87 L.Ed 1628 (1943).

Obscene material has been defined by the U.S. Supreme Court as "material which deals with sex in a manner appealing to prurient interest." Roth v. United States, 354 US 476, 487, 1 L. Ed.2d 1498, 77 S.Ct. 1304 (1957). In ordinary language, it is called pornography, derived from the Greek *porne*, harlot and *graphos*, writing.

Obscene material is not protected by the First Amendment and the states may outlaw its dissemination along with material that might fall short of obscenity but is deemed harmful to the juvenile population. U.S.C.A. Const.Amend. 1; Roth v. U.S. supra.

Miller v. California, 413 U.S. 15, 37 L.Ed. 2d 419, 93 S.Ct. 2607 (1973) became a true landmark case when the U.S. Supreme Court established a three-pronged test to determine what was obscene. By that test, obscene material must (1) predominantly appeal to the prurient, shameful or morbid interest; (2) be patently offensive to prevailing standards in the community; and (3) taken as a whole, lack "serious literary, artistic, political or scientific value." 413 U.S. at 24, 93 S.Ct. at 2615.

Miller was a departure from a prior test under which the third prong required that obscenity be "utterly without redeeming social importance" which was the standard established by Roth. This change was the result of what the Court considered the impossibility of the prosecution being able to establish a negative, an impossible burden under criminal standards of proof. 413 U.S. at 22.

Vulgar or obscene words or sentences cannot be considered in isolation. The work must be examined as a whole. Likewise, some small measure of literary merit cannot save what otherwise lacks literary value as a whole. "A quotation from Voltaire in the flyleaf of a book will not constitutionally redeem an otherwise obscene publication . . ." *Kois* v. Wisconsin, 408 U.S. 229, 231, 33 L.Ed. 2d 312, 92 S.Ct. 975 (1966).

THE PROBLEM OF JUVENILE MATERIAL

Prevailing standards have so driven back the boundaries of obscenity as to limit it to almost pure "hard core" pornography and

Bruce Strauch 113

present libraries with few worries in collection development. The more troublesome problem is dealing with juveniles in the pre-teen to seventeen year old range to whom many state laws prohibit dissemination of material that might otherwise be suitable for adults.

A recently challenged Virginia statute reads as follows:

Code sec. 18.2-391

UNLAWFUL ACTS. — (a) It shall be unlawful for any person knowingly to sell, rent or loan to a juvenile, or to knowingly display for commercial purpose in a manner whereby juveniles may examine and peruse:

1. Any picture, photography, drawing, sculpture, motion picture film, or similar visual representation or image of a person or portion of the human body which depicts sexually explicity nudity, sexual conduct or sadomasochistic abuse and which is harmful to juveniles, or

2. Any book, pamphlet, magazine, printed matter however reproduced, or sound recording which contains any matter enumerated in subdivision (1) of this subsection, or explicity and detailed verbal descriptions or narrative accounts of sexual excitement, sexual conduct or sadomasochistic abuse and which, taken as a whole, is harmful to juveniles.

The American Booksellers Association along with a variety of other publisher and periodical distribution associations brought suit for declaratory and injunctive relief in the United States District Court for the Eastern District of Virginia, seeking to enjoin enforcement of the statute. The statute was found unconstitutional, was appealed to the Court of Appeals for the Fourth Circuit, which affirmed the district court's decision and was appealed finally to the U.S. Supreme Court in 1988. By a relatively recent development in the law, the Supreme Court certified questions of Virginia law to the Supreme Court of Virginia, resulting in the caption *Commonwealth of Virginia v. American Booksellers Association, Inc., et al.*, 372 S.E.2d 618 (Va. 1988).

One of the major issues was the second prong of the *Miller* test. To be prohibited to minors, the material must be lacking "serious literary, artistic, political or scientific value" for juveniles. The fear of booksellers was that material would be outlawed because unsuitable for young children, although proper for older adolescents.

The booksellers submitted a list of books that they feared were "harmful for juveniles" within the statutory definition i.e., they contained detailed verbal descriptions or narrative accounts of sexual excitement, conduct and abuse.

- R. Bell, *Changing Bodies, Changing Lives* (1980)
- J. Betancourt, *Am I Normal?* (1983)
- J. Blume, *Forever . . .* (1975)
- P. Blumstein & P. Schwartz, *American Couples* (1983)
- J. Collins, *Hollywood Wives* (1983)
- A. Comfort & J. Comfort, *The Facts of Love* (1979)
- S. Donaldson, *Lord Foul's Bane* (1977)
- *The Family of Woman* (J. Mason ed. 1979)
- P. Haines, *The Diamond Waterfall* (1984)
- J. Lindsey, *Tender is the Storm* (1985)
- J. Joyce, *Ulysses* (1961)
- *The New Our Bodies, Ourselves* (J. Pincus and W. Sanford ed. 1984)
- L. Niven & J. Pournelle, *Lucifer's Hammer* (1977)
- *The Penguin Book of Love Poetry* (J. Stallworthy ed. 1973)
- M. Sheffield, *Where Do Babies Come From?* (1972)
- J. Updike, *The Witches of Eastwick* (1984)

The U.S. Supreme Court has never held that the community standard test should result in a measured majority dictating literary merit to the minority of the population, however discrete that minority might be. *Pope v. Illinois*, 481 U.S. 497, 107 S.Ct. 1918, 95 L.Ed.2d 439 (1987); *Pinkus v. United States*, 436 U.S. 293, 98 S.Ct. 1808, 56 L.Ed.2d 293 (1978).

Concurring with this, the Virginia Supreme Court had no trouble finding that work of serious literary or artistic, political or scientific value for a "legitimate minority of normal, older adolescents" could not be found lacking in value for the larger class of juveniles of all ages. *Commonwealth* supra at 624. The Court noted that the list of books had been well selected to range from classic literature to pot-boilers. Without reviewing the books in detail, they were found to pass the third prong of the test and not be harmful to juveniles.

The second question considered was the problem of prohibiting booksellers from allowing minors to peruse material they were otherwise unable to purchase.

The statute was directed solely at a "display for commercial purpose" and thus eliminated any risk for libraries. Still, a more rigorous statute could easily be imagined that would include libraries within its scope, making the holding of the court of some interest.

Peruse was defined as:

> To examine or consider or survey with some attention and typically for the purpose of discovering or noting one or more specific points: look at or look through fairly attentively: go through: STUDY . . ., READ . . ., to read through or read over with some attention and typically for the purpose of discovering or noting one or more specific points . . .

Webster's Third New International Dictionary 1688 (1976)

The statute was clearly intended to prohibit detailed examination and not just the quick glance or the survey of labels or covers on the shelves of the store. It is a criminal statute that required the state show beyond a reasonable doubt that the bookseller knowingly allowed juveniles to peruse the prohibited material or took no reasonable steps to prevent it. *Commonwealth* supra at 624.

The stealthy juvenile might sneak a look or even a quick study in the same way that he might shoplift and be undetected by the store owner. The burden was on the storeowner to take only reasonable steps to ensure that this did not happen.

While the question of "reasonable steps" is a jury issue dependent upon the circumstances of the case, evidence was presented that the statute would affect probably no more than a single shelf of the booksellers stock. It is typical to find the shelf of prohibited wares within sight of the clerk. The stealthy juvenile could be easily detected under those circumstances. The burden for the store was not very heavy at all.

The ABA has obviously achieved something, but it is not certain what. All the classic questions of what is obscenity still remain on a book-by-book basis. The Virginia Supreme Court passed on a list of fifteen books, many of which will soon be out of print. J. Joyce being dead, perhaps *Ulysses* is permanently in the clear. J. Collins, however, will doubtless have another saga of Hollywood out next year just packed full of "sexual excitement." Will the next book of J. Collins be suitable for older adolescents, and at what age does an "older adolescent" begin?

The U.S. Supreme Court has made it quite plain that obscenity will be judged at least for the first two prongs on a community standard, and that differing jury verdicts in different communities are acceptable under the law.

> It is neither realistic nor constitutionally sound to read the First Amendment as requiring that the people of Maine or Mississippi accept public depiction of conduct found tolerable in Las Vegas, or New York City.

> *Miller* supra 413 U.S. at 31
> 37 L.Ed.2d at 435

The majority of the Court would agree and reply, true, that is why the power is in the hands of juries throughout the land. Justice Douglas, however, questions the first principle and urges a constitutional amendment and legislative action to determine whether people want any censorship limits on obscenity at all. Indeed, it might be easier and more effective to simply restrict the sales locations of raunchy materials rather than worry about what is and is not obscene.

All these grand ideas aside, how is the library to respond to the state of the law?

1. There is clearly an obligation to pay attention to the state obscenity law and police the collection development within whatever crude guidelines are provided.
2. Juvenile access to the library must be supervised according not just to ordinary library procedure but in regard to what materials juveniles are permitted under the state obscenity law.
3. Libraries are not likely to have a "skin magazine" rack like bookstores that will be under the baleful eye of stern supervi-

sion. In libraries of open stacks where "unsuitable materials" as defined by the state obscenity law are mixed in with the general collection, a necessity may arise to restrict juvenile access altogether. This might even provide a handy excuse for college libraries fatigued with high school students roaming at will.

RELATED READING OF INTEREST

Action For Children's Television v. FCC, 852 F.2d 1332 (D.C.Cir. 1988) – FCC must give broadcasters clear guidelines for hours of channeling of indecent but not obscene material.

American Booksellers Ass'n. v. Hudnut, 771 F.2d 323 (1985) – a truly fascinating case in which the city council of Indianapolis attempted to define pornography as the "subordination of women" and allow any victim of injury by an assailant who has seen pornography a civil cause of action against the maker or seller of the pornography.

Catharine A. MacKinnon, *Pornography, Civil Rights, and Speech*, 20 Harv. Civ.Rts. – Civ.Lib.L.Rev. 1 (1985) – for a statement of the sociological basis of the Indianapolis obscenity theory.

FCC v. Pacifica Foundation, 438 U.S. 726, 98 S.Ct. 3026, 57 L.Ed.2d 1073 (1978). – FCC definition of indecent material in broadcasting including times of day in which children watch T.V.

Globe Newspaper Co. v. Superior Court, 457 U.S. 596, 102 S.Ct. 2613, 73 L.Ed.2d 248 (1982) – interest of the state in the minor.

Henkin, *Morals and the Constitution: The Sin of Obscenity*, 63 Colm.L.Rev. 391 (1963) – distinguishing between laws that impose morality on children and laws that support parents in teaching morals as they choose.

New York v. Ferber, 458 U.S. 747, 102 S.Ct. 3348, 73 L.Ed.2d 1113 (1982) – compelling interest of the state in safeguarding the "physical and psychological well-being of a minor."

U.S. v. Pryba, 674 F.Supp. 1518 (E.D.Va. 1987) – obscenity may not be presumed for all material in a smut shop where some of the material has been found obscene – burden on judge and jury to review all the material.

Claiming Periodicals:
The "Trembling Balance"
in the "Feud of Want and Have"

Barbara A. Carlson

SUMMARY. Although librarians and publishers approach periodical claiming from different perspectives, the process generally works because it is supported by a superstructure of ethical conduct. At times, however, stresses on the system, whether caused by internal or external forces, threaten to corrode the ethical boundaries. Before this point is reached, operations need to be systematically analyzed and understood from the opposite viewpoints then brought together as common concerns in order to solve problems in this mutually troublesome area of serials acquisitions.

The world is emblematic. Parts of speech are metaphors, because the whole of nature is a metaphor of the human mind. The laws of moral nature answer to those of matter as face to face in a glass. "The visible world and the relation of its parts, is the dial plate of the invisible." The axioms of physics translate the laws of ethics. Thus, "the whole is greater than its part"; "reaction is equal to action"; "the smallest weight may be made to lift the greatest, the difference of weight being compensated by time"; and many the like propositions, which have ethical as well as physical sense.

— Ralph Waldo Emerson, *Nature* [1836][1]

Just as Ralph Waldo Emerson wrote that compensation is a universal law of nature, the claiming of periodicals might be described

---

Barbara A. Carlson is Head, Serials Management, at the Medical University of South Carolina, Library, 171 Ashley Ave., Charleston, SC 29425.

in Emerson's words as part of a "trembling balance" in "the feud of want and have."[2] Claiming is really a delicate balance of compensation between librarians and publishers, which is supported by an ethical superstructure.

The polarity between the two participants is exemplified in the process, whereby sometimes adversarial positions are defined by occupational motivations. Librarians are driven by a service ethic and commercial publishers by the profit motive, both of which are justifiable. Despite the fact that there are fundamental differences at work, the process not only continues, but relies on unwritten, though understood, ethical boundaries among these and other constituents of the serials information industry. Thus, the invisible forces—the fair, just, good, and proper actions of both librarians and publishers—form the basis for solving the very practical and utilitarian problem of acquiring materials on subscription. In Emersonian terms, it is a proposition that has both ethical and physical senses and is a natural part of acquisitions.

Yet ethical activities can be, at the same time, the disruptive elements as well as the supporting structure in periodical acquisitions. Unfortunately, stresses on the normal operating procedures between these two parties often cause the system to work, much of the time, as a counterbalance between good-faith gestures and mutual distrust. They challenge and continuously disrupt the system and raise questions of behavior on ethical grounds. Strains on the claiming process are imposed by librarians, publishers, vendors, and other outside forces such as mail-delivery services. At times the system appears to break down and become contaminated with charges of dishonesty, incompetence, and irresponsible conduct, causing adversarial differences to dominate. Before this level is reached, arguments on either side which interfere with or prevent efficient operations need to be examined and understood from their own perspectives then brought together as common concerns, not by adversaries or unnatural allies, but by mutual dependents in the claiming process.

But what are the invisible forces, the ethical arguments on each side? When claiming periodical issues, librarians are guided by their codes of ethics as defined by their institutional and professional organizations. For librarians, a guarantee of the highest level of service and access to information drives them to demand receipt of complete journal subscriptions in an attempt to reduce user-frustration. As acquisitions officers representing the interests of their institutions and their users, they are ethically bound to be fiscally responsible in obtaining library materials. Journal subscription costs charged to libraries are significantly higher — sometimes two to three times those charged to individual subscribers. And so it follows that the monetary losses are greater if issues are not received and no compensation is forthcoming from the publisher. Also to be considered are the high-priced titles which rely on libraries for their circulation. For instance, if a library paid $1,370.00 ($1,268.29 list price plus $101.71 in added charges) for 20 issues of the *Journal of Immunological Methods* in 1988 and, hypothetically, failed to receive an issue, it recognized a loss of $68.50 plus the loss in staff time and salaries which accrued in claiming the issue. If such losses are multiplied by a number of subscriptions over a long period of time, the cost of acquiring periodical subscriptions becomes a nightmarish scenario rather than what it is generally perceived as a bad dream. Just like publishing companies, libraries are economically dependent institutions that cannot afford to waste resources. Periodical subscriptions pose a particular challenge to them because of prepayment terms for the long term receipt of items, whose deliveries are dependent upon international, national, and local mail services.

Quite conversely from that which dictates the actions of librarians, what drives the publishing industry is the bottom line in the budget. In the words of Robert G. Krupp, "It must never be forgotten that commercial publishers have truly only one realistic goal: to make a profit. This is not only understandable but acceptable by anyone with a sense of economics."[3] Claims are extremely costly to publishers and cut into their profit margins. They must overprint an economically viable percentage of each title in order to satisfy subscriptions and claims from subscribers as well as dedicate a substantial part of their workforce to customer services.

With both sides investing large amounts of time and money in claiming, let us look at the causes of claims by libraries. Often times librarians argue that claims are prompted by situations created by the publishers themselves. Besides the obvious need to claim for the receipt of skipped issues, libraries are forced to use claims in order to seek information and to clarify variables in publishing practices such as title changes, frequency changes, format changes, changes in publishing schedules, cessations, suspensions, mergers, splits, absorptions, numbering inconsistencies, combined issues, and printing defects. Claims are not only commodity-driven instruments but are communications instruments.

To better control their use in this way, when changes are warranted, publishers should clearly and precisely report such variables on issues preceding the change and distribute the information directly to their subscribers and to subscription agencies. Many publishers do report such changes via special mailings or through regular publications dedicated to such notices. By doing so in advance, they help prevent a flood of unnecessary claims. But not all publishers are so enlightened and an enforced industry standard to convey such variables is long overdue. To these publishing variables add the realities of smaller print runs and limited time restrictions on claiming, and the frustration level of librarians rises proportionally. Consequently, the money-is-the-root-of-all-evil syndrome is superimposed on the ethical identity of publishers by many librarians. They see themselves and their institutions as the victims of the villainous publishers who are motivated by greed and raise the cost of journal subscriptions to further punish libraries. At times, stress on the system appears to reach critical levels, although there has been better communication along these lines in recent years with the advent of direct electronic linkages between libraries, subscription agencies, and publishers.

Perhaps this is a good time for some additional comments concerning publisher claiming restrictions. Generally publishers have put time limitations on many of their titles whereby unless missing issues are claimed within a designated length of time from publication, they will not be honored free of charge. Usually if librarians have efficient and effective ordering, checkin, and claiming systems in place, whether manual or automated, these restrictions are acceptable and are not liabilities in acquisitions work. Most publishers will honor domestic claims within three to six months and foreign ones if claimed within six months to a year. If shorter timeframes are designated, for example, the two months for domestic and three months for foreign on some monthlies and bimonthlies by one well-known publisher, libraries can make adjustments accordingly. Publishers impose such restrictions because they cannot honor claims indefinitely. Their role as producers and suppliers of serial literature has boundaries as defined by the demand for back issue inventories, which are not generally profitable investments for them as corporations. There are times, however, when such restrictions appear to move beyond the realm of restrictive to being prohibitive as in the case of a 30-day maximum allowance for claiming. But in all fairness, it has been this author's experience that when claims on titles have been pursued within a "reasonable" time, they have been honored in spite of stated claiming restrictions.

Publisher claiming restrictions are attempts by publishers to operate their businesses more efficiently, and are not meant as punitive policies toward libraries. Realistically, they are measures imposed on libraries by publishers which encourage better management techniques in acquisitions.

Publishers know that subscribers, including libraries, are responsible for creating situations that prompt unnecessary claims, for example, late claims and late orders and renewals. Some statistics compiled by Elsevier from their Amsterdam office reveal that 7% of claims were received too late to honor free of charge and that 4% of claims were due to late orders or renewals.[4] Premature and late claims are costly to publishers and to libraries alike. Premature claims often result in the receipt of duplicate issues, which for libraries take staff time to manage and for publishers take profits. Duplicate issues may eventually just become unwanted, discarded items, a waste from both sides of the issue.

From the other perspective, as John Merriman writes, "Publishers maintain that a high proportion of missing issues arrive or are subsequently found, and for this reason some of them automatically reject first claims if, from their records, it appears that the copy was correctly sent."[5] To ignore first claims on immediate issues is the well-known policy of several major commercial journal publishers. Again, it is their way of dealing with costly premature claims, a defense mechanism against mismanagement.

But now let us venture into the realm of intentional mismanagement. A serious charge which has been a long-standing complaint is that librarians are issuing claims for periodical items that have been received but subsequently misplaced, stolen, or lost. This belief is part of the invisible, unethical undercurrent which undermines the process. It is apparent from a statement on or by the lateness of some claims that publishers receive them for issues when libraries go to bind volumes, consequently discovering an issue missing. It is perceived by publishers that such issues have already been received. Rightfully so, publishers are not responsible or obligated to replace free of charge such issues, and libraries must order replacement issues at an additional charge. Although generally thought of as an honest lot by publishers, librarians sometimes resort to such methods either out of desperation or lack of acquisition skills. It is sometimes felt that some librarians operate at the expense of publishers, and, it is obvious that some are actually guilty of doing this. Under the present delivery systems, it is difficult to prove that a library received the item even though the proper address is on record. More often than not, publishers will honor such claims, although suspicions of unwarranted claims fuel mistrust. In the words of Huibert Paul, who as a librarian and one time assistant editor of *PNLA Quarterly* has seen both sides of the feud:

> The publisher is not always to blame, nor is the mailman. While it is probably true that the majority of claims from libraries are genuine and the issues indeed never were received, there must also be many cases where issues arrived but simply got lost in the library itself. I do not know how otherwise to explain some of the complaints I have received about missing issues. It has also happened that a library has claimed nonreceipt of the last four or so issues while we could find nothing wrong with our mailing list.[6]

However, in all fairness, there may be instances when the existence of issues that do not fit into the normal publishing sequence, such as supplements or special issues, is not discovered until the volume is pulled for binding, the index is checked, or a request from a library user is received. Such crisis claiming is prompted by irregular publication schedules.

Another serious allegation: Publishers charge librarians with claiming prematurely and excessively, especially now that automated serials control systems make it easier for them to perform claiming operations. Charges of unethical and irresponsible behavior on the part of some librarians with automated systems that alledgedly have been dumping unreviewed claims onto agents, who in turn dump them onto publishers, are running rampant in the serials community, and is even supported in theory (since it is as yet unproven) by fellow librarians whose systems are still unautomated. Once again, villains are designated through innuendo and generalizations, a situation which only tends to polarize and splinter the system. Instead of counter-productive rumors, systematic analyses of in-house library systems must be mandated by the serials community in order to best measure the impact that automation is having on periodical claiming, proving or disproving the charges. This author reported on such a study in a paper presented at the annual meeting of the Medical Library Association in Boston in May 1989,[7] and encourages fellow librarians to evaluate how responsible their serial claiming operations are managed.

Automation has only increased the dilemma for librarians – the need to claim promptly but not prematurely. Have librarians demonstrated any real management skills in the area of claiming which would reinforce their ethical backbones in the eyes of publishers? Premature claims by automated systems seem to be causing few problems for the larger commercial publishers because of the earlier mentioned policy to ignore them and, in fact, may indeed be helping to better manage early fulfillment of unreceived issues. What seem to plague large and small publishers alike are libraries which claim and claim and claim the same titles relentlessly time after time. Such activity does not go unnoticed or unrecorded by many publishers and agents.

The stress of using mail-delivery systems adds further to the growing ethical debates. Technically, and in general, the rules and regulations governing the mail delivery of periodical subscriptions favor the publisher rather than the library. The regulations of the Federal Trade Commission offer serial librarians little legal support in fulfilling their fiscal obligations concerning periodical subscriptions. Trade Regulation Rule Chapter I, Part 435, of CFR Title 16 governs commercial practices on mail order merchandise protecting the buyer with a continuous option to cancel and receive a prompt refund when notified by the seller that the merchandise cannot be supplied within a specified time. However, this rule only aids librarians in acquiring certain issues. It states "this part shall not apply to subscriptions, such as magazine sales, ordered for serial delivery, after the initial shipment is made in compliance with this part."[8] The regulation treats periodicals as though they were fixed entities such as materials in book format and limits the librarian's legal means of recourse beyond the initial shipment.

Perhaps this explains in part why the forces which govern such subscription agreements primarily are not looked upon by librarians as legal contractual agreements but as financial commitments based on good-faith gestures between professions. Or is this reliance on an ethical superstructure between members of the information industry representative of the library community's naive sense of business practices? It is generally recognized that journal publishers make the rules and set the terms which libraries are expected to follow and comply, regardless of the consequences, and there are no litigations on record by libraries which have challenged publishers on uncompensated loss of dollars and resulting gaps in holdings when replacement copies could not be obtained. Only when librarians become better informed consumers, demonstrate professional managerial skills, and show greater astuteness toward legislation that impacts on their activities will they be able to have a more equitable, and influential, say in the want/have equation. Until such a time, they will remain in the eyes of many in the disadvantaged position, relying on the goodness of the serial suppliers.

Perhaps both librarians and publishers should reflect on the words of Emerson's good friend, Henry David Thoreau. "If two travelers would go their way harmoniously together, the one must take as true and just a view of things as the other, else their path will not be strewn with roses."[9] Claiming is one area in which serials librarians and publishers need to look from the other's point of view and work together to devise appropriate checks and balances. In this thorny arena of serials acquisitions, the actual structure of the claiming process needs reinforcement and work from both sides. Procedures — the physical — must be reviewed from the two perspectives but with the common goal of making the system work with positive, ethical support.

REFERENCES

1. Ralph Waldo Emerson. *Nature, Addresses and Lectures*. First AMS ed. New York: AMS Press, 1968, p. 32-33. (Reprint of Riverside Press Edition issued as v.1 of the *Complete Works of Ralph Waldo Emerson*, Boston: Houghton, Mifflin & Co., 1903)
2. _____. "Compensation." *Essays*. Boston: Houghton, Mifflin & Co., 1883, p. 89.
3. Robert G. Krupp. "Issues in Acquisition of Science Literature." In *Special Librarianship*. Edited by Eugene B. Jackson. Metuchen, N.J.: Scarecrow, 1980, p. 492.
4. John Tagler, Director of Marketing Services, Elsevier Science Publishing Company, Inc. to Bobbie Carlson, Head, Serials Management, Medical University of South Carolina, 3 May 1989 [letter].
5. John B. Merriman. "The Work of a Periodicals Agent." *Serials Librarian* 14, no. 3/4 (1988): 28.
6. Huibert Paul. "The Serials Librarian and the Journals Publisher." *Scholarly Publishing* 3 (Jan. 1972): 182.
7. Barbara A. Carlson. "Guilt-Free Automated Claiming." *Serials Review* 15, no. 4 (1989): 33-42.
8. *Code of Federal Regulations*. Vol 16, 1977, Part 435. *Federal Register*, v. 40, no. 205, Wednesday, Oct. 22, 1975, p. 49493.
9. Henry David Thoreau. *A Week on the Concord and Merrimack Rivers*. Edited with introduction and notes by Walter Harding. New York: Holt, Rinehart & Winston, 1963, p. 238.

Stretching the Acquisitions Budget by Negotiating Subscription Agency Service Charges

N. Bernard "Buzzy" Basch
Judy McQueen

SUMMARY. Within the context of rising serials costs, this article explores ways that acquisitions personnel might be able to negotiate lower service charges levied by subscription agencies.

Librarians are acutely aware of the impact of soaring serial prices on acquisition budgets. But, while the cost of journal subscriptions and the rise in publisher prices have been the focus of many articles and meetings, little attention has been paid to subscription agency service charges. Protests about publisher prices have little impact on the cost of serials. However, a library can achieve significant and immediate reductions in subscription agency service charges — charges that can consume as much as six percent of a library's annual serial expenditures — by negotiating with its vendor.

A successful negotiation — one that brings a fair return for both parties — requires knowledgeable participants. As the party that stands to gain the most immediate returns from a negotiation — cost reduction — the library must assume the responsibility for educating the negotiators: preparing its own staff, and gathering information to be shared with the vendor. For the vendor, the benefits of negotiation — a loyal and committed customer base — are less tangible, take longer to mature, and may be difficult to perceive in the face of immediate reductions in account income.

Buzzy Basch and Judy McQueen are independent consultants based in Chicago, IL.

In order to identify realistic negotiating opportunities, the serials manager needs an understanding of subscription agency operations, including costs and the variables included in service charges. The negotiation must focus on approaches with the potential to reduce library costs *without* reducing essential services, and *without* putting the agent out of business.

The factors that affect agency service charges include: the mix of titles to which a library subscribes; the subset of agency services used by the library; the formula the agency uses to calculate service charges; and the value of money, the cost of labor, and economies of scale in agency operations. An examination of each of these factors in a specific library-agency relationship can provide a number of points for negotiation to reduce service charges.

The mix of titles to which the library subscribes is important because each title represents a different cost and income equation for the agent. Agents receive discounts from some publishers. The discounts vary for different titles and different types of material. An agency can offer significantly reduced service charges on lists which include many titles with high publisher discounts. The potential for economies of scale in agency operations make it advantageous for a library to present its complete list for negotiation — the titles handled by the agent, those handled by other agents, and those ordered direct.

A library's service mix — the number and type of subscription agency services used by the library — is also of significance. Review the library's use of each of the agency's services: ordering, claiming, library-specific data entry, standard and special reports, online system usage, continuations and standing order processing, serials check-in services, serials control systems, machine-readable bibliographic data and invoicing, custom automated system interface, one-time and recurring charges, and the like. A library manager alert to the range of the vendor's services and the importance of each to the library will be better positioned to appreciate the impact of services essential to the library — the maintenance of multiple ship-to and billing addresses, for instance — on the supplier's costs and to see the opportunities for negotiation when a library makes minimal or no use of a "standard" service that entails considerable supplier expense. Similarly, a comparative knowledge of the practices of vendors can provide leverage for negotiating a reduction in the price of a service that other vendors offer for a lower price or for no direct charge-back.

Although rarely mentioned, most subscription agencies follow a formal approach in calculating the service charge on an account. Some use a precise formula with variables covering specifics such as the title and service mix, and a gross margin. Others use the concept more loosely, expressing the service charge as a dollar amount or a percentage on the average line item on an invoice or the library's total list.

In preparation for a negotiation, the manager should review the library's subscription lists and the vendor's invoices for the past three years. Examine *all* invoices: not only the annual invoices, but also those for additional titles ordered, bill-backs, "bill later" titles, and separate invoices for price increases and continuations. Prepare separate totals for subscription prices and service charges, and calculate the service charge as a percentage of the subscription cost. The results can be surprising—to both the librarian and the vendor—sometimes revealing a service charge level significantly higher than documented on the annual invoice. If the library uses more than one supplier, a comparative analysis can prove illuminating but not necessarily conclusive, as the mix of titles placed with each supplier may be significantly different, as may the library's use of the services offered by each agent.

A further perspective can be obtained by comparing the library's service usage and charges with those of other institutions with similar collections, serviced by the same or different vendors. Such information can be assembled by a series of "last minute" phone calls, but the picture will be more reliable if this aspect of serials costing is monitored continuously—at meetings and through informal contact with colleagues.

An awareness of the importance of cash flow and the value of money in the vendor's business cycle can provide opportunities for negotiation. Agencies pay publishers in advance of subscription start dates, but they also invoice libraries well in advance of publisher payment deadlines. Libraries which pay promptly upon the receipt of an invoice provide agencies with significant cash resources. A payment received in June can be invested for several months before it has to be drawn on to pay the publishers. With a prime rate of 11 percent, a four month investment has a value of 3-2/3 percent. Negotiating to deduct this 3-2/3 percent from an annual invoice can reduce a four percent service charge to one-third of one percent.

Time is money, at least in relation to labor charges. Most agencies offer vendor submission of claims as a standard service. Claim preparation is labor intensive. Libraries that submit all claims directly to the publisher, those which are not able to identify material that requires claiming and thus do not submit claims, and those that use their own staff to enter claims into an agency's electronic system, all save the vendor money. These savings may not be directly translatable to lower service charges, but may be sufficient to trade for other benefits such as free access to the vendor's electronic claiming system.

Like libraries, subscription agencies have many fixed costs — rent, computer systems, catalog production, etc. There is a clear advantage in assigning such costs over the largest possible base of orders. Agencies are responsive to arrangements that increase the number of orders handled without adding significantly to the costs of obtaining and maintaining these orders.

There is usually a point where the service charge structure is such that it is less expensive for a library to order a title direct from the publisher than through an agent, the costs of the library's processing of the order being lower than the agent's service charge for the title. Some agents seek to prevent attrition by agreeing to a ceiling on the service charge levied against any single title. The most frequently quoted ceiling is around $30. On an account with an average service charge of four percent, the $30 ceiling cuts in on titles with a subscription price of $750. Recognizing that agents want to maintain or increase the number of orders processed, a library with a number of expensive titles can usually obtain both a ceiling on the service charge for these titles and further benefits, simply by agreeing to place such orders with the agent. Differential discounting policies by overseas publishers make foreign titles an appealing profit center for subscription agencies, providing libraries with lists rich in such titles with similar opportunities.

Likewise, an undertaking to consolidate all the library's orders with a single agent can be a valuable bargaining point, as can the period for which a library commits its subscriptions to the vendor. Over five years, a $50,000 account maintained with a single vendor represents a $250,000 order. An account with little change in the title mix requires minimum maintenance, resulting in lower vendor costs for second and subsequent years.

An awareness of the importance of such factors in agency operations, a considered statement of a library's service requirements, an organized approach to negotiation, and a commitment to the philosophy of providing a fair return for good service can lead to a library-vendor negotiation that is a win-win situation for both parties. The library can achieve significant savings in serial subscription service charges, the agency gains a loyal and knowledgeable customer.

The exchange of views and give and take inherent in a negotiation are most readily achieved through a formal face-to-face meeting between the serials manager and the vendor's representative. However, some of the same results can be obtained through a formal bid process *if* the library undertakes similar research and ensures that the bid document reflects both its service and price needs and the realities of the vendor's business requirements.

The Ethics of Library Discard Practices

Rosann Bazirjian

SUMMARY. This paper explores the issue of ethics in relation to library discard practices, and attempts to address the weeding process from a philosophical point of view. An overview of some of the origins of ethical theories, including those of Kant, Epicurus and Epictetus, is given and related to college library weeding practices. Moral obligation is a key phrase when considering the concept of ethics. Honesty, objectivity, competency, and loyalty as they relate to the moral obligation most libraries have to keep their collections current, is examined. It is argued that these concepts do indeed substantiate the assumption that discarding is an ethical practice. Ethics has long been an area of concern to the American Library Association. An analysis of the professional status of librarians and the concept of ALA Codes of Ethics is addressed in this paper in order to place the issue in historical perspective. Finally, the issue of ethics versus law, and where discarding/weeding practices fit into that scheme, is discussed.

There are many reasons for weeding library collections. Some of them are justified while others are not. Since these reasons have been stated before, I will refrain from repeating all of the same old cliches. But, have we as librarians ever considered the ethical implications of the term "discards" or the significance of our actions when we discard titles? Is discarding an ethical practice? Why do some of us love throwing those books away, and others absolutely disdain it? Our strong feelings, one way or the other, are based on

Rosann Bazirjian is Head of Acquisitions/Coordinator of Collection Development, at the University of West Florida, John C. Pace Library, 11000 University Parkway, Pensacola, FL 32514.

something we feel internally. These feelings stem from our conscience and are called ethics.

DEFINITION OF ETHICS

How do we define ethics? Ethics deals with what kinds of actions are right and wrong or good and bad, with the final judgement residing in an individual's conscience. What ought or ought not exist is measured by internal standards rather than by outside forces and is a result of individual belief. When the derivation of the word "ethics" is traced, one finds that it originally meant character, as opposed to intellect.[1] Attributing something to character and not intellect unconsciously gives it less credibility. Consequently, we are inferring that our actions stem from our emotions rather than from our minds.

Other aspects of the term ethics include professional conduct and moral obligation both to one's self and society. The forces which keep our actions within bounds are public opinion or personal conscience, both of which are in direct opposition to political law or state power. We measure our sense of what is right and wrong by internal standards, not by a standard which has established legal criterion. As a result, we must be careful when considering the weeding process. Exploring the ethical issues involved in discarding practices used by libraries leads to an explanation of the way we feel about "de-selection" and from where these feelings originate.

PHILOSOPHICAL THEORIES OF ETHICS AND THE COLLEGE LIBRARY

Tracing the varying theories of ethics throughout the generations, a very interesting thread emerges. Historically, philosophical theories seem to substantiate the assumption that discarding is definitely an ethical practice. The following are highlights of some of the major philosophical theories related to ethics.

The utilitarian view of ethics states that the goodness of the consequence is what matters, and makes something ethically right. The philosophy of "goodness" is also an element of the philosophy of

Immanuel Kant. Immanuel Kant (1724-1804) was a deeply critical philosopher whose profound thoughts led him to concentrate on science and its foundations. Kant believed that it is the goodness of one's motives which makes something right; that the mind orders all of our experiences; and that man's conscience reveals that moral precepts are necessary and valid. Our motives in discarding are to rid the library of superseded and damaged material and to make the library a dynamic place not one grown stiff in the joints. Many organizations do not meet their established goals "because of internal decay and rigidification."[2] As Frederick Wezeman so aptly states, "the cheapest, most effective, but often least used piece of library equipment is the wastebasket."[3] Kant postulated that the rational nature of man is the basis for morality. Applying this theory to discarding library materials, a rational, organized approach to weeding can be viewed as truly ethical.

The idea of happiness and serenity of life was the primary concern of Epicurus (342-270 BC). He theorized that ethics meant achieving a thorough knowledge of the nature of things and that only this knowledge would rid one from superstitions and fear. If we understand why we discard and why the process is so beneficial, all the fears of making mistakes, or the superstitions about tossing out "sacred" items will disappear. Epicurus analyzed pleasure by arguing that it is the healthy condition of a being. Pleasure, he felt, should serve as the objective goal which determines our actions resulting in overall organization in our lives. The condition of "divine invulnerability"[4] can exist if we rid all contingency from our lives and through pure reasoning reach happiness and self-sufficiency.

A Roman stoic, Epictetus (336-264 BC), believed that it is the wise individual who limits his desires to what is within his reach and understands what is within his power, and that moral individuals live according to the dictates of reason. Applying this belief to our profession, college libraries need to understand exactly who they serve and the purpose of their collections and should not be striving to imitate those larger research libraries who perhaps might not need to weed their collections. If, as Epictetus believes, it is the attitude toward events rather than the events themselves which make something ethical, then our approach to discarding becomes all important.

IS DISCARDING GOOD?

What role then, if any, does ethics have in the discarding or weeding of library materials? We can start out very simply by asking the question "Is discarding good?" To discard. Webster's definition of discard is to "get rid of as useless or unpleasant."[5] Examine the words we use when discussing the "retirement" of titles from a library collection. Common expressions are purging, destroying, "out the back door," and trashing. We have inherited a negative connotation of what is a beneficial and necessary library function. The guilt we feel when "purging" our library collections merely gives this negative feeling credibility. Could we look upon discarding as an art, as a process which requires the same skill and competency as is needed in book selection or acquisition? If the answer is "yes," then is discarding "good"?

To many who study philosophy, the end result is what makes something good or bad. Would most people approve of standard discarding practices if they knew of the consequences? What are the theories underlying this practice? Discarding, or weeding, keeps book collections current, creates room on shelves for new titles, assures that patrons are receiving the most current information possible, removes damaged materials from our stacks, and eliminates multiple entries for a particular title from our computer files. Do these ends justify the means? Achieving the educational goals of a university or satisfying the needs of students in terms of collection development should be enough to answer this question with a "yes." Some philosophers, however, argue that a course of action is good only if it is approved by the majority of the people. When the consequences of a good weeding program are made public and the reasons why we discard materials support our own ethical opinions, then hopefully we have a satisfied clientele and our ethical judgments begin to direct others' opinions rather than merely describe them. A characterization of "goodness," then, leads to favorable interest, or so we hope.

MORAL OBLIGATION

The phrase moral obligation involves many components including: honesty, objectivity, competency, and loyalty. How one defines these will determine just how ethical library discarding practices appear. The conscience also plays a major role in determining our moral obligations. It is said that conscience is "the author of and the authority for our moral obligations."[6] Our conscience is what prompts us to perform our duties and in a sense becomes the supreme authority which makes us moral beings. Furthermore, the conscience acts as the regulating agent of our behavior and is the code which resolves conflicting personal and social interests. Everyone finds what is right inside of himself and this determines the moral code that he follows.

Moral Obligation: Honesty

The characteristic of honesty is closely related to conscience. Honesty is being truthful to oneself as well as to those you serve. Do we believe that the discarding of titles improves the quality of a library collection, or are we of the school of thought that believes that the "book not owned is a greater loss to some potential user than is one book too many?"[7] Library patrons are better served by the very best and current collection of books a library can offer. The term "library" is not synonymous with "museum." Other than certain primary sources and classics, the undergraduate library should not be housing "relics." Libraries only hurt the patron and possibly present him or her with misleading or even wrong information when outdated texts fill the shelves. A library patron is not helped by that outdated text he or she inadvertently picks up because he did not notice that the last line of the call number was 1972 and not 1989. Not only would the frustration factor for patrons be reduced, but library usage would in all likelihood increase due to the inspiration of accurate, timely information easily located on the library shelves. As librarians, we have an obligation to be aware of our clients' needs in relation to current curricula. It is important to take a careful look at the library collection to make sure it has indeed changed with "the times," since a library shelf full of outdated material gives the library user a bad impression of the institution.

In terms of a library collection, honesty involves the willingness to give items up. As Frederick Wezeman states, "how much support would the parks department receive if it permitted the golf courses to be overrun with weeds."[8] Dead titles are not only expensive to house, but also hinder a library's goals as well. In a time when so many libraries are running out of physical space, the need to weed our collections becomes ever more critical. One should not rely on alternatives such as physical library expansion or the presence of CD-ROM. Physical expansion requires funding which is not always available, and many libraries are not yet prepared to discontinue paper copies in favor of the as yet "unproven" CD-ROM technology. Although Interlibrary Loan, which makes one library's resources available to another library, is an alternative which might make the thought of discarding a bit easier, libraries must honestly make the necessary decisions to discard some materials.

Moral Obligation: Objectivity

Objectivity is another moral obligation. So much of ethics involves mental dispositions such as personal taste and subject matter biases. The professional who remains objective could be considered cold-hearted or uncaring. Can the librarian remain objective when selecting titles for discard? Does one discriminate when considering items on a title by title basis? It is important that librarians remain impartial and always base discarding decisions solely on criteria valid for their particular institution. As Seneca said, "Let us train our minds to desire what the situation demands."[9] The assessment of what is to be discarded should be based on user needs, not individual taste. Such is the idea of ethics which is based upon shared interests. Discard decisions should be based on what is best for our clientele, else, the action would indeed be unethical because it would take into consideration an individual's beliefs rather that the interests of all the patrons. The existentialist view of ethics is that nothing, not even God's will, can relieve an individual of having to make choices and decisions; no universal principles can sanctify what we decide. We are responsible for actions that are under our own control and need to make discard decisions based on objectivity and professional judgment. Objective knowledge frees one's mind from error and emotional conflict. This ethical theory expressed by Spinoza, says that one could never make a mistake if one remains objective.

Some would argue that it is difficult for librarians to remain objective when it comes to books. Books are often regarded with awe as sacred objects and we are taught as children to love books and treat them carefully. We give books lifelike characteristics by calling them our "friends," and it is difficult to discard old "friends." Many books have specific memory associations for some individuals, and might even remind us that time goes by so quickly. We are used to discarding Pepsi cans or Coca Cola bottles, but certainly not books. However, as Howard F. McGaw so aptly said, "If a book is not needed, it is only paper, ink, cardboard, and cloth, ready to be junked."[10] Again, it becomes significant to remain above individual conscience and strictly adhere to required criteria.

Moral Obligation: Competency

Moral obligation also involves competency. When librarians are hired, it is assumed that they will fulfill their job assignments, and be trusted to do what is in the library's best interests. Trust is earned by the competent librarian; by the individual who honestly explains the significance of his actions; who supports his decisions; and who remains true to his or her beliefs. "A professional's obligation to a client are those necessary to deserve the client's trust that these activities will be performed in a manner to promote the client's interests."[11] Patrons need to trust librarians to do what the patron wants, as well as to do what we are hired for. A conservative approach or that old-fashioned squirrel instinct are not in the best interests of the undergraduate library. One must remember that the potential for discarding grows stronger every year a book sits unused on a library shelf. "It is the sign of a healthy condition of the book collection and a wise administration of the book fund when the library's annual report reveals a fair correspondence between the number of new books regularly purchased and the number of books regularly discarded."[12]

Moral Obligation: Loyalty

A final component of moral obligation is loyalty. The concept of loyalty takes motives and intentions into consideration. As librarians, we shape and determine our book collections and service policies by molding the library into what we feel, in conjunction with our administration, is the most efficient way to operate. We make the library work and we make it either good or bad. Loyalty to the university's goals, to our administrators' beliefs, and to our patrons needs is part of what makes us professionals. The loyalty to our book collections is what should be leading us to discard. We want the best collection we can have, and that can only be accomplished through a steady weeding practice.

AMERICAN LIBRARY ASSOCIATION AND ETHICS

A review of the literature reveals that the topic of ethics has been a concern of the library profession for some time. Since 1929, the American Library Association has considered adopting official statements on ethics; however, even the final draft in 1981 remains of little significance to the profession. Unfortunately, many librarians are unaware that a "Code of Ethics" exists. Ethical codes are well established for many professions, most notably those in law and medicine. Perhaps the lack of a well-publicized ethics code for librarians is why we are sometimes referred to as "semi-professional." "In some contexts, the term professional librarian simply means adequately trained."[13] As William J. Goode continues to say, the librarian is viewed as a "gatekeeper" and "custodian of the stock."[14]

Without a resolute ethical code, the profession encounters difficulty in obtaining the necessary respect and trust from its clientele. How then can the profession exert an influence or impose authority on its clients? Only when the librarian works within the patrons' demands rather than imposing his or her own, can a bond of respect and trust be established. "The public believes libraries, but not librarians, are important. At present, the librarian has little power over his clients."[15] Does discarding become an even greater stumbling block in terms of patron emotions when it is the library that is important, more so than the librarian's actions?

The librarian becomes a professional once librarianship attains the stature of a profession. To do that one must understand that one needs to serve the interests of society even if his or her decisions are not popular, i.e., discarding books. Librarians who view their roles solely as disseminators of information rather than as responsible decision makers hurt the profession. Unfortunately, the librarian's sense of obligation to serve sometimes hinders doing what is best for the institution. Because we are not always viewed as a profession, our patrons believe that it is their right to complain about things such as overdue fines and even book discard practices. Librarians know that our policies and practices are determined by our values; however, because of our "semi-professional" status, we can state reasons but not prove them to be correct. "Thus, the librarian accepts the task of facilitating the implementation or achievement of standards of excellence whose definition and custodianship belong to others. In the university library, the others are the professors."[16]

This is exactly why we take extra, time-consuming steps when we want to discard books. Some of us provide faculty members with a list of every title about to be withdrawn for their review, others surreptitiously take their books to the dumpster ten or more blocks away just so no one "catches us," and of course, we must remember to remove those covers and all markings that indicate that we ever owned the book. Wouldn't it be so much simpler if respect for our profession was so strong that there would be no question that what we selected to discard was right?

Until our profession is allowed to influence its constituency it will not be granted any sort of stature. Until it is understood that librarians possess professional skills, that we create the order in the library which makes it a valuable place to study and learn, we will be considered nothing more than custodians guarding the book collection. The ability to function effectively, with objectivity and honesty, in harmony with ethical values, is essential to professional performance.

ETHICS AND LAW

In this day and time, a review of ethics relating to the discarding of library books must also include the relationship between ethics and law. Whereas ethics deals with perfecting an individual's character, law tends to concentrate on an individual's relation to other men. The authority of law lies within the "external manifestations"[17] of these relations, rather than to what is confined in an individuals mind, which is ethics. There is a common meeting ground between law and ethics in that the rules of ethics that determine our inner thoughts will influence these "external manifestations" as well.

As mentioned earlier, ethics is determined by public opinion, whereas law is enforced by political codes. But, let's think about this connection. When we discard material from libraries, we need to be politically careful lest the faculty notice the dumpster nearby. When a group such as the faculty strongly oppose library discard practices, a force called public opinion emerges. If that opinion is very strong and long lasting, it will "eventually crystallize into law."[18] It might only be the university's law, but nonetheless it is just as binding and possibly just as restrictive.

Librarians working at state universities are also confronted with legal issues when making discard decisions. Books are purchased with state funds, therefore making them state property paid for by taxpayers' money. Do we, as librarians, have a legal right to discard material purchased with state funds? Many state institutions are free to offer their discarded material to other non-profit institutions or to various international programs sponsored by the university. The ultimate disposition of withdrawn materials from state institutions that cannot be placed elsewhere is extremely complicated, and the true laws governing their disposition vary from state to state. Consequently, librarians need to be very competent, diligent, truthful and politically careful when participating in a weeding procedure.

CONCLUSION

The following is a quotation from Oliver A. Johnson's book entitled *Ethics: Selections From Classical and Contemporary Writers*. "Actions are right in proportion as they tend to promote happiness, wrong as they tend to produce the reverse of happiness."[19] In other words, what is right for one may be wrong for another, and it is not possible to please all of the people all of the time. In short, we all have our own beliefs by which we judge others' actions to be either good or bad, or right or wrong. We all follow our own moral theories and try to eliminate from our lives all conflict or question of those theories. If we can begin to understand the reasons behind our moral judgments, we will then be taking the first step toward seeking an ethical theory answering the question, is discarding library books ethical?

REFERENCES

1. Geo. W. Warvell, *Essays in Legal Ethics*, Littleton, CO: Fred B. Rothman & Co., 1980. p. 3.

2. Laurence J. Peter, *Peter's Quotations*, Toronto: Bantam Books, 1977. p. 267.

3. Frederick Wezeman, "Psychological Barriers to Weeding," *Bulletin of the American Library Association*, 52 (8) (September 1952): 638.

4. Phillip Mitsis, *Epicurus' Ethical Theory: The Pleasures of Invulnerability*, Ithaca, NY: Cornell University Press, 1988. p. 1.

5. *Webster's New Collegiate Dictionary*, Springfield, MA: G & C Merriam Company, 1974. p. 324.

6. Ethel M. Albert, *Great Traditions in Ethics*, Belmont, CA: Wadsworth Publishing Co., 1984. p. 169.

7. Arthur Curley and Dorothy Broderick, *Building Library Collections*, Metuchen, NJ: Scarecrow Press, 1985. p. 308.

8. Frederick Wezeman, *op. cit.*, p. 639.

9. Laurence J. Peter, *op. cit.*, p. 274.

10. Howard F. McGaw, "Policies and Practices in Discarding," *Library Trends* 4 (3) (January, 1956): 271.

11. Michael D. Bayles, *Professional Ethics*, Belmont, CA: Wadsworth Publishing Co., 1989. p. 74.

12. Howard F. McGaw, *op. cit.*, p. 276.

13. William J. Goode, "The Librarian: From Occupation to Profession," *Library Quarterly* 31 (4) (October, 1961): 312.

14. *Ibid.*, p. 313.

15. *Ibid.*, p. 316.
16. *Ibid.*, p. 318.
17. Geo. W. Warvelle, *op. cit.*, p. 11.
18. *Ibid.*, p. 15.
19. Oliver A. Johnson, *Ethics: Selection from Classical and Contemporary Writers*, New York: Holt, Rinehart & Winston, 1965. p. 239.

BIBLIOGRAPHY

Albert, Ethel M. *Great Traditions in Ethics*. Belmont, CA: Wadsworth Publishing Co., 1984.

Bayles, Michael D. *Professional Ethics*. Belmont, CA: Wadsworth Publishing Co., 1989.

Curley, Arthur, and Broderick, Dorothy. *Building Library Collections*. Metuchen, NJ: The Scarecrow Press, Inc., 1985.

Evans, G. Edward. *Developing Library and Information Center Collections*. Littleton, CO: Libraries Unlimited, Inc., 1987.

Goode, William J. "The Librarian: From Occupation to Profession." *Library Quarterly 31* (4) (October 1961): 306-320.

Hauptman, Robert. "Overdue." *Wilson Library Bulletin 50* (8) (April 1976): 626-627.

Johnson, Oliver A. *Ethics: Selections From Classical and Contemporary Writers*. New York, NY: Holt, Rinehart and Winston, 1965.

Lindsey, Jonathan A., and Prentice, Ann E. *Professional Ethics and Librarians*. Phoenix, AZ: Oryx Press, 1985.

McGaw, Howard F. "Policies and Practices in Discarding." *Library Trends 4* (3) (January, 1956): 269-282.

Mitsis, Phillip. *Epicurus' Ethical Theory: the Pleasures of Invulnerability*. Ithaca, NY: Cornell University Press, 1988.

Peter, Laurence. *Peter's Quotations*. Toronto: Bantam Books, 1977.

Peterson, Kenneth G. "Ethics in Academic Librarianship: the Need for Values." *The Journal of Academic Librarianship 9* (3) (January 1983): 132-137.

Reed-Scott, Jutta. "Implementation and Evaluation of a Weeding Program." *Collection Management 7* (2) (Summer 1985): 59-67.

Stueart, Robert D. "Weeding of Library Materials – Politics and Policies." *Collection Management 7* (2) (Summer 1985): 47-58.

Tong, Rosemarie. *Ethics in Policy Analysis*. Englewood Cliffs, NJ: Prentice-Hall, Inc., 1986.

Warvelle, Geo. W. *Essays in Legal Ethics*. Littleton, CO: Fred B. Rothman & Co., 1980.

Webster's New Collegiate Dictionary. Springfield, MA: G & C Merriam Company, 1974.

Wezeman, Frederick. "Psychological Barriers to Weeding." *Bulletin of the American Library Association 52* (8) (September 1952): 637-639.